Bible Interpretations

Fourth Series

April 3-June 26, 1892

Psalms and Daniel

Bible Interpretations

Fourth Series

Psalms and Daniel

These Bible Interpretations were given during the early eighteen nineties at the Christian Science Theological Seminary at Chicago, Illinois. This Seminary was independent of the First Church of Christ Scientist in Boston, Mass.

By

Emma Curtis Hopkins

President of the Christian Science Theological Seminary at Chicago, Illinois

W<small>ISE</small> W<small>OMAN</small> P<small>RESS</small>

Bible Interpretations: Third Series

By Emma Curtis Hopkins

© WiseWoman Press

Managing Editor: Michael Terranova

ISBN: 978-0945385-54-7

WiseWoman Press

Portland, OR 97217

www.wisewomanpress.com

www.emmacurtishopkins.com

CONTENTS

	Foreword by Rev. Natalie R. Jean vii
	Introduction by Rev. Michael Terranova ix
I.	REALM OF THOUGHT .... 1 *Psalm 1:1-6*
II.	THE POWER OF FAITH .... 12 *Psalm 2:1-12*
III.	LET THE SPIRIT WORK .... 21 *Psalm 19:1-14*
IV.	CHRIST IS DOMINION .... 27 *Psalm 23:1-6*
V.	EXTERNAL OR MYSTIC .... 37 *Psalm 51:1-13*
VI.	VALUE OF EARLY BELIEFS .... 47 *Psalm 72:1-9*
VII.	TRUTH MAKES FREE .... 55 *Psalm 84:1-12*
VIII.	FALSE IDEAS OF GOD .... 65 *Psalm 103:1-22*
IX.	BUT MEN MUST WORK .... 74 *Daniel 1:8-21*
X.	ARTIFICIAL HELPS .... 83 *Daniel 2:36-49, Revelations 12: 7, 8*
XI.	DWELLING IN PERFECT LIFE .... 93 *Daniel 3:13-25*
XII.	WHICH STREAK SHALL RULE .... 104 *Daniel 6:16-28*
XIII.	SEE THINGS AS THEY ARE .... 117 *Review of 12 Lessons*
	List of Bible Interpretation Series 134

Foreword

By Rev. Natalie R. Jean

I have read many teachings by Emma Curtis Hopkins, but the teachings that touch the very essence of my soul are her Bible Interpretations. There are many books written on the teachings of the Bible, but none can touch the surface of the true messages more than these Bible Interpretations. With each word you can feel and see how Spirit spoke through Emma. The mystical interpretations take you on a wonderful journey to Self Realization.

Each passage opens your consciousness to a new awareness of the realities of life. The illusions of life seem to disappear through each interpretation. Emma teaches that we are the key that unlocks the doorway to the light that shines within. She incorporates ideals of other religions into her teachings, in order to understand the commonalities, so that there is a complete understanding of our Oneness. Emma opens our eyes and mind to a better today and exciting future.

Emma Curtis Hopkins, one of the Founders of New Thought teaches us to love ourselves, to speak our Truth, and to focus on our Good. My life has moved in wonderful directions because of her teachings. I know the only thing that can move me in this world is God. May these interpretations guide you to a similar path and may you truly remember that "There Is Good For You and You Ought to Have It."

Introduction

Emma Curtis Hopkins was born in 1849 in Killingsly, Connecticut. She passed on April 8, 1925. Mrs. Hopkins had a marvelous education and could read many of the worlds classical texts in their original language. During her extensive studies she was always able to discover the Universal Truths in each of the world's sacred traditions. She quotes from many of these teachings in her writings. As she was a very private person, we know little about her personal life. What we do know has been gleaned from other people or from the archived writings we have been able to discover.

Emma Curtis Hopkins was one of the greatest influences on the New Thought movement in the United States. She taught over 50,000 people the Universal Truth of knowing "God is all there is." She taught many of founders of early New Thought, and in turn these individuals expanded the influence of her teachings. All of her writings encourage the student to enter into a personal relationship with God. She presses us to deny anything except the Truth of this Spiritual Presence in every area of our lives. This is the central focus of all her teachings.

The first six series of Bible Interpretations were presented at her seminary in Chicago, Illinois. The remaining Series', probably close to thirty, were printed in the Inter Ocean Newspaper in Chicago. Many of the lessons are no longer available for various reasons. It is the intention of WiseWoman Press to publish as many of these Bible Interpretations as possible. Our hope is that any missing lessons will be found or directed to us.

I am very honored to join the long line of people that have been involved in publishing Emma Curtis Hopkins's Bible Interpretations. Some confusion exists as to the numbering sequence of the lessons. In the early 1920's many of the lessons were published by the Highwatch Fellowship. Inadvertently the first two lessons were omitted from the numbering system. Rev. Joanna Rogers has corrected this mistake by finding the first two lessons and restoring them to their rightful place in the order. Rev. Rogers has been able to find many of the missing lessons at the International New Thought Alliance archives in Mesa, Arizona. Rev. Rogers painstakingly scoured the archives for the missing lessons as well as for Mrs. Hopkins other works. She has published much of what was discovered. WiseWoman Press is now publishing the correctly numbered series of the Bible Interpretations.

In the early 1940's, there was a resurgence of interest in Emma's works. At that time, Highwatch Fellowship began to publish many of her writings, and it was then that *High Mysticism*, her seminal work was published. Previously, the material contained in High Mysticism was only available as individual lessons and was brought together in book form for the first time. Although there were many errors in these first publications and many Bible verses were incorrectly quoted, I am happy to announce that WiseWoman Press is now publishing *High Mysticism* in the a corrected format. This corrected form was scanned faithfully from the original, individual lessons.

The next person to publish some of the Bible Lessons was Rev. Marge Flotron from the Ministry of Truth International in Chicago, Illinois. She published the Bible Lessons as well as many of Emma's other works. By her initiative, Emma's writings were brought to a larger audience when DeVorss & Company, a longtime publisher of Truth Teachings, took on the publication of her key works.

In addition, Dr. Carmelita Trowbridge, founding minister of The Sanctuary of Truth in Alhambra, California, inspired her assistant minister, Rev. Shirley Lawrence, to publish many of Emma's works, including the first three series of Bible Interpretations. Rev. Lawrence created mail order courses for many of these Series. She has graciously passed on any information she had, in order to assure that these works continue to inspire individuals and groups who are called to further study of the teachings of Mrs. Hopkins.

Finally, a very special acknowledgement goes to Rev Natalie Jean, who has worked diligently to retrieve several of Emma's lessons from the Library of Congress, as well as libraries in Chicago. Rev. Jean hand-typed many of the lessons she found on microfilm. Much of what she found is on her website, www.highwatch.net.

It is with a grateful heart that I am able to pass on these wonderful teachings. I have been studying dear Emma's works for fifteen years. I was introduced to her writings by my mentor and teacher, Rev. Marcia Sutton. I have been overjoyed with the results of delving deeply into these Truth Teachings.

In 2004, I wrote a Sacred Covenant entitled "Resurrecting Emma," and created a website, www.emmacurtishopkins.com. The result of creating this covenant and website has brought many of Emma's works into my hands and has deepened my faith in God. As a result of my love for these works, I was led to become a member of WiseWoman Press and to publish these wonderful teachings. God is Good.

My understanding of Truth from these divinely inspired teachings keeps bringing great Joy, Freedom, and Peace to my life.

Dear reader; It is with an open heart that I offer these works to you, and I know they will touch you as they have touched me. Together we are living in the Truth that God is truly present, and living for and through each of us.

The greatest Truth Emma presented to us is "My Good is my God, Omnipresent, Omnipotent and Omniscient."

Rev. Michael Terranova
WiseWoman Press
Vancouver, Washington, 2010

LESSON I

REALM OF THOUGHT

Psalm 1:1-6

Here in this first Psalm, we have a lesson in contrasts. The mental processes starting from the choice of the will, or the choice of the affections, gather ideas on their way, and are confronted by and by with the results of holding those ideas they have chosen.

It is not at all necessary that one should think as his neighbors do, nor that he should think as things and circumstances around him would like him to. He may think what he pleases. And what he pleases to think will make up his destiny of human experience.

One may insist upon thinking lightly of misfortune till his mind becomes so buoyant and joyous that he has actually lost the power to be downcast or depressed. Then, of course, he will draw to himself people and circumstances and affairs buoyant and joyous. For we draw a "congregation" (as it is here called) of things about us exactly like our mind.

As the magnetized bar draws steel filings, so does your determination to be cheerful draw cheerful conditions. This is as true of the wretch in the slums as of Victoria. This is the gospel. Not admitting any idea that can draw misery as its outshowing, one might come up out of the most depressing situations like a cork out of water.

Mark Antony said: "But I, unless I think what has happened is an evil, am not injured. And it is my power not to think so." So the psalmist tried to paint the discomfort of the mind that chooses to think how dark the world is, how dishonest people are, how unfortunate innocent creatures are. It is an idea of his that you can scare people into being good by painting the torments of the bad. It is a wrong notion. For if you cause the mind to imagine anything, the body and surroundings will scramble to carry out the imagination.

Many times children are imagined to be doing something, or to have been doing something, which they had never thought of. They stand out as expressions of our ideals, and feel a masterful impulsion to carry out our imaginations. So the next thing we hear of is that they are doing just as we imagined. Then we praise ourselves for our intuitions. Nay, let us cleanse us of unrighteousness rather, for we pushed them into the doing. We thought and they acted as:

"My friend and I were lovers;
It was good for us to be together.
We were companions in our trust;
But one day I suspected him - my friend,
Of doing that which he had not.
I did not tell him of my suspect,
But his unconscious eye looked grief.
I kept on still suspecting him, while he was innocent,
Till by and by he looked askance at me,
And was afraid when I was nigh.
And I went on still holding my gnawing worm of suspect,
While he, my friend, was innocent,
Till by and by he caught the word
That haunted me, and it tempted him
To do that which in my heart I thought.
He tremblingly went towards the action,
I all the while determining he had done it,
Till in an evil hour my friend,
Who formerly was innocent,
Was guilty of the deed I had thought in my heart.
And now he walks a sinner
Who erstwhile was righteous,
Made sinner by my suspect
Who, my God, is guilty in this case –
My friend who once was innocent,
Or I who thought him guilty?"

When one thinks oppositely of friends, children, events, purposely, on principle, one can get his mind so trained that it will never walk in the "counsel of the ungodly." It is not in the slightest necessary for anyone to think anyone or anything is not good. When one sees how a man ill uses another man, a prompt metaphysical process will cause his hand to drop and his heart to forget even its intention to do wrong. The fountain of kindness and nobility will spring forth. This fountain is the living spring within everyone and everything. Our thoughts have been part of the rubbish covering men and women and children and things. To remove our thoughts is to take off part of the rubbish.

In the Science of Mind we find what thoughts have most potency at removing rubbish.

We need to keep ourselves free from the rubbish of false notions. The second lesson in Spiritual Science deals entirely with the process of self-cleansing — setting free. The only thing to be rid of is one's own thoughts. These thoughts are gathered from people very often. Take the man lying on his bed of sickness. What put him there? Thoughts. Whose thoughts? Those his neighbors gave him, that his family gave him, those he has imagined on his own account.

The neighbors' thoughts lie down on him like dead weights. They say, "You must not sit up. You must not eat. You must not drink. You must have this done. You must have that done." On what compulsion must he? If he will think within his mind, "I put away your ideas, they are nothing to me; I am able to do what I please," very soon he will rise buoyantly out of their notions, and even they will admit that he is right. He need not open his lips. Mind is master. If he should say that aloud, he would get into controversy which would irritate them all. He would make more work for his mind. No need of piling Pelion upon Ossa (famous Greek mountains, therefore mountain upon mountain), to get free from his ailments. To get to thinking as other people do, is to "walk in their counsel." The mind walks around among the kingdom of thoughts not seen by the eyes nor heard by the ears. Just as we are celebrating the discovery of America, another unknown kingdom spreads its angled wiles and wonderful rivers before our gaze. It is the kingdom of thoughts. To understand thoughts, is to understand things. Everything is made up of thoughts, governed by thoughts, moved by thoughts. We ought to have someone arise with a genius for managing thoughts. Only one has ever understood the realm at all. That was Jesus of Nazareth. The rest have been trying to understand it. They have improved sufficiently to ward off those wild ideas which make sickness. They are hastening so as not to be at all afraid of the thoughts of their neighbors.

That is a great advance on the fears they had not so very long ago that other people's thoughts were bad for them. They are rousing to understand dominion over conditions of all kinds now. The knowledge that *"Thou wilt keep him in perfect peace whose mind is stayed on Thee"* (Isaiah 26:3), is the call to understand how to have peace by taking the right staff as we walk through to this country.

We get to "sitting in the seat of the scornful" by thinking that there is so much greed among rich men that there are starving millions for us to be anxious about. This scorn is not healing for bruises. There is an idea that is healing for bruises made by the grasping and over-reaching of the men of the world. Ignore the physical shadows dropped down by thoughts, and put over the country of causation the right idea. Here it is: "I pronounce all greed and dishonesty finished — ended. The Good now reigns supreme."

Pay no attention to material things that look impossible to be ended. The God whose word spoken is the redemption of all hearts said definitely; *"Thou shall decree a thing and it shall be established unto thee"* (Job 22:28).

This giant idea sent stalking through the realm of mind will knock down every thing not like itself. The man who had thought of cornering the wheat says, "I shan't do it; I can not." The woman who was trying to get the advantage of her customer stops suddenly. The man who was sick with discouragement lifts up his head. He goes out and finds a position. Your giant cleared his mind's eye and sent him straight to the right place.

In this realm of mind, it was said by one who traveled over a certain patch thereof, that it is possible for one to shut his eyes and stop his ears so entirely to what is going on in the streets and in houses, as to hear the voice of the King saying:

"This is the way," and then, that everyone who so hears will go right into the line of prosperity.

By the understanding of causes and how to govern causes, we find the way to our own prosperity. By the knowledge of Truth, we discover that everyone has his own way of being prosperous. There is prosperity for every creature. It will not come by worldly dodges nor indeed by following out the lines of theology announced by the most popular preachers. It seems hard to tell this Truth. It looks as if one were trying to speak ill of good preachers. No, it is good to tell what is true. It is good news to say that you need not believe one word about hades or satan, or the dispensation of Providence, or the visitation of God through sickness, weakness, death, calamity, poverty. All those things are the shadows cast by ideas. Change the ideas and the real dispensations of Providence and visitations of God will shine like the smiles of those you love best. The rich revivings that come with the ideas are here likened to "Trees planted by rivers of living waters." This is like the talk of Jesus Christ. He said: *"To him that hath, shall be given; and from him that hath not, shall be taken even that he seemeth to have"* (Matthew 13:12).

The Scriptures are a unit in telling that you attract more and more of things and people and powers like your thoughts. Both these texts prove this. If you keep your mind on prosperity, you will have that idea enrich and revive as a tree planted by living waters, or, as Jesus Christ said, more *"shall be given to him."* So then, what little idea of misery he did have or you did have, will drop away. *"From him shall be taken that which he seemeth to have."*

Here we are told to stand in judgment and also in the congregation of the righteous. Our thoughts are our "congregation." We must stand up and hold our own with our own congregation. The platform on which we stand is God, the life of the universe. It is not the will of God that anyone or anything should ever die. Did you ever make the erroneous statement, "It has pleased God to cause our good brother to be taken from us?" Well, now, your judgment has not been exercised by such a lie. It has leaned against nothing and so when your child or mother was exposed to your presence, she felt faint.

Tell your congregation of thoughts that the great poets and theologians may enjoy their sicknesses, misfortunes, disappointments, if they please; you propose to have some judgment of your own. So you say: "My God is the Giver and Keeper of the life of all things. He never sends death to anything or anyone. Hearing cannot end. Light cannot fail. Peace is unbroken. Joy is endless. Buoyant vigor is increasing. This is my kind of God." As this is the true God, you cannot have any of the dying gifts of that old imaginary being your judgment used to lean against.

Your congregation will revive with your words. That is, every idea that you have will be happy and vigorous. Then your acquaintances will grow healthy. Every old person is a trait of yours that is getting towards its end. Notice the peculiarity of him or her and see your odd conceit standing forth. Every lame person is the walking image of one of our ideas. Get well grounded in the four propositions of metaphysics or Spiritual Science, and you will cure lameness. These are the four propositions. They are better than anarchy, or nihilism, or want, unrest, hate.

1) "It is not God's will that anyone or anything should ever be sick or diseased; God is the health of the universe. 2) It is not God's will that anyone or anything should be feeble or weak; God is the strength of the world. 3) It is not God's will that anyone or anything should be hurt or frightened; God is the defense of the world. 4) It is not God's will that anyone or anything should ever know want; God is the support of the world."

[margin note: the 4 propositions]

This is a lesson in will. While you are silent, with the wills of millions of creatures determined to get their advantage whether you are advantaged or not, crossing and recrossing over you like a network, look calmly, coolly, at the situation.

You cannot manage all those wills by any will of yours bent on the same purpose. This is what Jesus Christ meant by saying, *"I can of mine own self do nothing"* (John 8:28). The will that is like that network of wills is quite unequal to the Herculean task of fighting them. Breathe deep now. That will lies deep. Your breath is your dominion.

There is a will that is God. It is your true will. It will snap all those wills crossed over and against you. Now choose deliberately the true ideas of God to live by and you will find life will completely change. That will is acting. Sometimes you may say, "I can do nothing with these things. Jesus Christ can manage them easily. To Jesus Christ I leave them."

As Jesus Christ is within you, you will probably do or say something yourself which will be strong, positive, dominant. Yet the old-fashioned domineering human will, will not be in your words or actions. It is Jesus Christ's will speaking and acting. Jesus Christ is dominion. *"Be not afraid,"* *He said, "I have overcome the world"* (John 16:33). There have been people so feeble they could not sit up, who breathed their breath deep-clear to the foundations of their body, knowing that the breath was dominion, and they burned as with fires while the hot blood tingled through them. Then they arose new creatures. This was after many people who did not believe in the breath of dominion, but did believe in the breath of death, had given them up.

The will that keeps so still is the silence of God, waiting to rise like the lion of the tribe of Judah, with your word. "Without the word was nothing made." You yourself are the Word. You speak when you please. You speak what you please. The psalmist notices how miserable people are who look at human experience with the idea of meeting it with human methods. He also speaks of the conquering shouts of those who ignore the wills of the world and speak from the deep places where the Omnipotent Will within us all rests. It rouses like a strong lion from its lair. To all the purposes of the world set against life, health, strength, judgment, supplies, it says, "It is finished. The kingdoms of this world are now become the kingdoms of our Lord and His Christ."

April 3, 1892

Psalm 1:1-6 Blessed is the man that walketh not in the counsel of the ungodly, nor standeth in the way of sinners, nor sit in the seat of the scornful. 2 But his delight is in the law of the Lord, and in his law doth he meditate both day and night. 3/And he shall be like the tree planted by the rivers of waters, that bringeth forth his fruit in his season; his leaf also shall not wither; and whatsoever he doeth shall prosper. 4/The ungodly are not so; but are like the chaff which the wind driveth away. 5/Therefore the ungodly shall not stand in the judgment, nor sinners in the congregation of the righteous. 6/For the Lord knoweth the way of the righteous: but the way of the ungodly shall perish.

LESSON II

THE POWER OF FAITH

Psalm 2:1-12

Before noticing today's lesson, make the connection in this course which last Sunday's text suggests. That can be summed up in the four propositions distinctly announced by the Psalm (2nd) explained esoterically.

They are these:

(1) I stand by the Omnipotent Truth that God is the Life of Omnipresence and as God is Life without any death there is therefore no death at all to Substance or Strength.

To believe in death is to be what this psalmist denominated a "heathen imagining vain things." By this statement we come into clear knowledge of what the eastern sages meant by saying thousands of years ago that:

> *"He who thinks that he can slay a life,*
> *Or he who thinks life can be slain, these both do err;*
> *For life is God, and God cannot be slain."*

We understand that it is as great an evidence of heathenism or ignorance to strike down one's neighbor with intent to slay as to preach that it is wicked to kill, or vice versa. For there is only one Life in the universe. It fills the universe full. There is no place to take life from and none to take it to, save itself.

The outshowing of belief in death is the raging of anger, man against his brother man, supposing that his brother has gotten something away from him; or against fate, thinking ("imagining") we have been defrauded of something. We are here shown that *"according to thy faith be it unto thee"* (Matthew 9:29) is wholly in reference to human experiences. Faith is here shown to be that persistent way of thinking which is peculiar to every man, woman, child as distinct from his neighbor. It is what we think within our hearts independent of our speech and independent of our true Spirit, which determines our destiny.

For illustration, take Napoleon Bonaparte; he was always calculating what he should do in case he were defeated. This was his persistent thought. He was not born for defeat. There is a spring of the conquering Spirit buoyantly rising within the bosom of every child. It was so buoyantly near the surface in the little Napoleon that at six years of age he would fearlessly fight with boys twice his age and always whip them, because he had not then begun to calculate what he should do in case of being himself whipped.

He who knows the laws of the esoteric as related to the exoteric, will easily trace the teaching that *"as a man thinketh in his heart so is he"* (Proverbs 23:7), is written on the scroll of Napoleon's destiny. By and by that subtle river encroached upon the firm intent of his victorious mind, and though his voice was as rallying and his limbs as agile and energetic as ever, the time for the fruitage of his secret thoughts had come, and nothing could stay the signal and irredeemable defeat of Waterloo.

"What we are by thought was wrought and built." The belief that "man is born to die" will show forth in death. But death will not be true because we believe in death by any manner of means. Would it make any difference to the fact of there being a principle of righteousness if you should say that you did not believe in righteousness? It would change your conduct and darken your hopes, but that right is right would go right on regardless of your nonsense. So Life Omnipresent goes on forever filling all the spaces of Omnipresence with the living God though all the kings and preachers of the world proclaim how real death is.

In standing to pass along this first spiritual teaching of this psalm, rejoice in the discovery that it has an exoteric or practical effect to speak this great truth forth as a conviction of mind. Those who speak it as real conviction act as if they had been pushed into the current of living instead of struggling across it. Life flows visibly through them. Their blood bounds as if some obstruction had been suddenly removed. Their ears quicken, and the hearing they had supposed was dead they find to be as alive as in the days of boyhood before the mind had calculated about death.

Many a supposed dead faculty is waiting for the honest conviction of the mind, that this is true, viz., that all death is an imagination; all old age is the winding up of much believing in the reality of corpses, and all paralyzed or stopped faculties are the hints of truth that the persistent imaginations of mind are marshalling their forces. Imaginations show forth to all those who believe them. Sometimes those who are called Spiritual Scientists are scolded and abused for having death near them which they do not seem to be able to stop. Do you suppose Napoleon's sudden declaration, "I do not now believe in defeat," would have worked with sudden success against the marshalled armies of his years of mental calculation of defeats? No. Only the fires of the faith of God Himself work with instantaneous demonstration.

If you should look straight past all exteriors into the persistent expectations of death and calculations about death which those young faithists (called Spiritual Scientists) have, you would see their calloused minds striving to believe in life, but solidly determined upon death since their childhood. It is for the fire of God-faith, the cold mind yearns. God does not believe in death. So Jesus

THE POWER OF FAITH   Fourth Series

Faith is a persistent way of thinking.

said, *"Have the faith of God"* (Mark 11:22). Paul said, *"By faith the dead are raised."* He means that faith, which is the way the mind persists in thinking, will make life visible where it has been hidden by "heathen imaginations."

(2) The second proposition here made, as you will see by reading the first twelve verses of the Psalm, is: *"God is the health of the universe. As God is the Omnipresence, that which is not God is the nowhere present. As disease, imperfection, sickness are not God, they are nowhere present."*

This reminds us of Plato's saying, that when we "discover the one in the many, we have penetrated to the secret of existence." This proposition is universal. As the mind throws its free reasoning afar towards the horizons of the infinite seas, it feels the splendor of this truth that in Omnipresent Holiness, there is no imperfection, and if the mind is honest and docile, it will know that as we live in God, breathe in God, and move in God, so for us also there is no sickness or disease, or imperfect substance. *I live in God; I breathe in God; I move in God.*

That which is true of the large is true of the small. That which is true of the all is true of the one. All and each may say truly, "What God is, that I am." Just as soon as this wholesome doctrine gets the consent of the secret heart, the cheeks redden, the flesh glows, the breath deepens. "I am well." Here we are brought to face the question of where God is, and we must bring

The persistent faith of the woman who touched the hem of Jesus' garment was her persistent thought that He had the power to heal her. She persisted to the point of Risk-taking & settling for a touch of his robe! Her faith was in His faith! Mercy! Thy faith hath made thee whole! what is my persistent thing?

Science, revelation, and practical experience to confirm one another.

It is according to the Science of Christ that for the lightest word we give a demonstration. The text is, *"For the lightest word thou shall give account."* The Science teaches that the words of Truth are *"Life to them that find them and death to all their flesh."* Revelation came to the spiritual hearts of the Brahmins ages ago, that "It is by the divine word that the sick are surely healed." Whoever speaks Truth with his secret heart in league with it, is healed. Let experience teach you. The experience of thousands upon thousands testifies that Truth is a healing principle. The cheery refreshment of Eternal Truth comes sifting its perfumes of youth and vigor through the tangled threads of our substance, and the promise is fulfilled. *"Thy light shall break forth as the morning and thy health shall spring forth speedily"* (Isaiah 58:8).

Is the Substance of God here? Yea, God is here. Is the Substance of God there? Yea, God is there.

Early in the study of the Science of God the students said, "We must look for God without us. We must think of Spirit as exterior, there, beyond; never within us." The practical effect of that divorcing of the without from the within in the thoughts of the heart was that while as a ministry they performed much healing of their neighbors, and made bold to dictate to the universe its mission as the substance of God, they were remarkably unable to cure themselves of their ailments. Palsy, blindness, lameness, pain kept their relentless hold upon them. Then there arose a message among them that, as their own substance was Spirit or God, they must look within for God, never without. They practiced according to the injunction over the Delphic temple — "Know thyself."

The practical results of this insistence upon the God within and not without was to make their eyes keen of sight, their bodies sound and wholesome; but they had not so much effect upon their neighbors' bodily health or physical faculties, and they were always finding their experiences with men and things and affairs disastrous.

They divorced the God substance within from the God substance without. Looking back over the history of mystic or religious teachings, we see that all divorce of every sort and kind sprang forth from the one-sided message, "God is within me, not without me," or "God is without me, not within me." All wars are the belief in divorce externalizing, the belief of life apart from Life. There was an ancient sage who made the beautiful announcement, "There is no apartness." They who do not believe in apartness will never have their homes broken by death or divorce or infidelity. They will never fear accidents or hurts or calamities. They will see their safety in the depths of the seas in their mother's home. *"Is he not yonder in the uttermost sea? The sea is His, He made it"* (Psalm 95:5).

(3) They will easily receive the third proposition of this psalm, which interpreted is, *"God is the defense, the protection, the surety of the universe, and as in God there is no danger, so in the universe where God abides, there is no danger forevermore."*

This is a Truth. Do you know what Truth has power to do when it is spoken? It can still the tempest, stop the earthquake, intercept the lightning, ward off accidents. Truth is Omnipotence. "On Truth the worlds were founded. By Truth the worlds were made. Truth is Lord over all and there is nothing higher than it."

If you dare to turn your mind's eye over the accidents and calamities of the ages, you are what this psalmist holds in derision as not having learned that imaginations of evil bring experiences of evil. How can evil be in the substance of God? Maimonides said, "When thy senses affirm what thy reason rejects, deny the testimony of the senses and listen to reason." Truth is reason. "God is our omnipresent defense forever." To say this will prove it. "There shall no ill come nigh thy dwelling."

(4) The fourth proposition that can be demonstrated as Truth is here brought out as, *"God is the support, the provider of the universe and all things in it. As God is the substance of all things and God is self-providing, nothing can want or lack or famish in all creation."* So many, who imagine lack,

want, indebtedness, poverty, should speak this truth? They must learn it by rote and have it for the secret run of their hearts till they forget that they ever imagined such idle tales as the failure of their substance.

Where it says here that we must *"Kiss the Son lest He be angry,"* it means that we must greet all creation as good to us. There is nothing to hurt us or rob us or defile us. Greet all things as God — as the Son, or message of God to us that even the stones tell us where there is gold with which to buy bread. The beasts call the direction from whence our success comes quickest. This moment the winds whisper the secret of our prosperity. Everything tells of universal bounty for each creature.

Love them. Condemn them not. It is as our mind secretly thinks that our world returns His dealings to us. But though we create our experiences by our mind's subtle thoughts, we do not create Truth. Forever these propositions which this psalm repeats woo us to speak them till God in His love is visible, not hidden. God is Truth, Truth is God.

April, 10, 1892

LESSON III

LET THE SPIRIT WORK

Psalm 19:1-14

This Nineteenth Psalm causes us to listen to every voice and watch every action as a message from Jehovah full of truth and inspiration for us.

The influence of taking literally such writings as this has always made people inspirational. To such a one upon hearing the propositions of Spiritual Science stated, while the mind was exercised to its highest point of perception of its message and instruction, the great conviction came that "Christianity as taught today was never the Truth of God nor the Truth of Life, and that the Science called Christian can never galvanize into the living faith of mankind the lifeless hoax, but out of its approximate truths the true doctrine can spring."

"Day unto day uttereth speech." It is the eternal renewal of Truth. When one speaks from honest conviction after much study of religious teachings, his highest conclusion is that Christianity as at present taught, and as understood by the early church fathers, and explained by the latest phase thereof, was never the Truth of God nor the Truth of Life, — we will listen. For only so far as a religious faith can practicalize, is it worth while. And only so far as it demonstrates what we all recognize as Good, is it true.

There must have been some total misconception of Truth in the minds of the early church fathers to have resulted in such savagery as they exhibited toward women and children. There must be some total misconception of Truth in the minds of those church people who are keeping such savage watch over the actions of that little child lest it steal, or overeat, or be too joyous. It must be some total misconception of Truth in the minds of those metaphysical exponents of Christianity who are sick, lame, blind, unfortunate. Let us be meek and lowly, and reason together to drop our faults, though in so doing we drop our seeming virtues. We will not pride ourselves on our piety or moralities while we are not manifesting the works of Jesus Christ.

There certainly are doctrines enunciated by Jesus Christ which are not now taught as He meant them. He was Spirit and His words were Spirit. He taught a spiritual doctrine in words suited to lift each grade of mind a step higher "day unto day." The profoundest mystic will find himself outstripped by the mysticism of Jesus. The most formal Puritan burning with pious self-righteousness his helpless neighbors, will find a text easy to interpret: "Do good. Forgive."

There have been certain works laid great stress upon in the most practical interpretations of Christianity. Those works are healing, teaching, reforming, raising from death. There have been certain ideas insisted upon as true, viz., that faith in God is necessary to our well-being; that understanding of God would make man one with God; that praise and thanksgiving to God would cause the heavens to drop down blessings. All these ideas are the rounds of Jacob's ladder to us. We take them and rest on them just long enough to spring on to the higher round.

While at first there was great stress laid upon the practical fruits of right faith, healing from sickness and reforming from vicious habits were looked for as necessary "evidences of Christianity." This was a higher round of the ladder of thinking than that one where we thought ourselves very well pleasing to God to accuse Him of sending us sickness and buffetings of Satan.

Then it was a higher round of the ladder of thinking when they who were healed and reformed refused to stop at such simple demonstrations, and boldly proclaimed that no one ever need be poor, no one ever need be hurt, no one ever need make any mistakes.

It was still a higher round when we were taught that a line of thinking would place us so in line with righteousness that we could be health and peace and bounty to all the world with whom we should come in contact without even trying to help them. It is still a higher round of the ladder of glory for the feet of our mind to stand upon, to proclaim that there never was any healing to be done, never any suffering to ameliorate, never any sins to pardon, for "there is no speech nor language where the voice of God Himself is not heard," exactly as the mystic sense of this psalm proclaims. And so when one tells us that it is no use to try to galvanize into life the miracles of Christianity, we understand him as meaning it is Christlike to declare there never was any necessity for miracles because God is all.

When one tells us that it is nonsense to teach that faith and praise and prayer are keys into the favor of God, we understand that it is truly Christlike to proclaim that Truth is true and Good is good whether we have faith in it or not, or whether we praise it or not. It is the highest doctrine of the rounds thus far, that we are already in heaven in the glory that was ours from the great forever without beginning of years or end of days. The higher the round one steps his thoughts upon, the more delightful he finds life.

"The sun" is always the headlight of Truth in these lessons. It has a "tabernacle." That is, there is always a place where someone speaks fearlessly one higher statement than is popular in his age. It is the sum total of all the teachings of the ages which interprets aright the Moslem marching song, "There is no God but God." It causes you to give up your former idea of God and to think not at all of God, but simply to rest while He thinks for you. It is the mind that ceases to project any thoughts at all which makes itself a vacuum into which Truth rushes.

While we are projecting our imaginations we are describing unrealities, because while we are projecting our thoughts, we see only our own creations.

"There is no understanding of errors," as it tells us here in the twelfth verse. There is only stopping our thinking. The great vacuum of silence, of stillness, of ceasing from thoughts is suction for the strength and understanding of God. He who stops thinking is greater than he who thinks the highest doctrines he has ever heard. He who does nothing is the greatest of workers. He lets God work. He who loves nothing and no one is the greatest lover, for he lets God love. He who wills nothing is the divinest demonstration of will, for he lets the will of God be done. This is Science. It is Revelation. It is practical. Rest from seeing will give your eyes strength of sight. God is rest. Rest from thinking will demonstrate perfection of Mind. God is Mind.

One who was writing of the Rest of God as revealed by John on the isle of Patmos felt the material objects of his room moving away from him; felt the ideas of his mind slipping from their cells into the abysses of nowhere; felt the rush of the Shekinah (Spiritual Presence) of God through his being; heard himself called by his own name as it is written in Paradise.

They who watch the quarreling of nations may watch no longer, *"In such an hour as ye think not Jesus Christ cometh"* (Luke 6:40). Let drop your notions of responsibility. God is the responsible. Let fall your imaginations of duties awaiting your efforts. God is the worker.

This is the Divine baptism of the water of life. Keep still. Stiller yet. Far stiller than the world ever thought of. It is now the hush of the morning of God. Now each one can be sure in himself, I do not work, I am worked. I do not think, I am thought. I do not will, I am willed. I do not love, I am loved. I do not move, I am moved. I do not need, I am needed. *"I came not to do mine own will, but the will of Him who sent me"* (John 5:30).

As I let the true will be done, I see heaven opening and the angels of God feeding the hungry, healing the distressed, exposing the souls of mankind, all white and gentle. As I keep still, I find that all heaven is contained in the doctrine of *"Let."* This is the mystic influence of the Nineteenth Psalm.

April 17, 1892

LESSON IV

CHRIST IS DOMINION

Psalm 23:1-6

Is this explanation of the Scriptures common? No. The Scriptures are usually described as lessons preparing mankind for a future state, instead of as actual information of immunities from every sort and kind of misery here and now.

The psalm reminds us of Daniel in the den of lions unharmed. How could Daniel be so safe in the lion's den? Because, as it is explained in (Daniel 1:4), he had *"understanding of Science."* What Science was that which Daniel, Hananiah, Mishael, and Azariah had? The Science of Om — Omniscience. They had great wisdom in this Science. Is that Science understood in our time? It is understood just so far as those studying it can save themselves from drowning by their understanding of Spirit, and not by their ability to swim or build rafts; by their safety in the midst of fires and swords through their knowledge of God, and not by their ability to run or fight back; by their never knowing pain, or sickness, or poverty through having the "Lord for their Shepherd."

What does it mean to have the Lord for a shepherd? It means having the law of the Spirit in the understanding so that material processes count for nothing. Can that law be understood now? Law of Spirit is eternal. Is this law in any respect like the law of matter and evil? *"My ways are not your ways"* (Isaiah 55:8), saith the Lord.

Why was not the thorn removed from Paul if understanding of Spirit redeems one from trouble? There was no thorn to remove. If Paul persisted in imagining a trouble and in declaring that he was able to bear a trouble, he would find himself able to bear his imagination. *"By thy words thou art justified"* (Matthew 12:37), saith Jesus.

Then it is not noble to endure great sorrows and afflictions with fortitude? It is the nobility of one who sets up a straw image and fights it, or of one who builds a pond of iced blood and walks through it, praising himself for his ability to endure cold and pain. Would it be nobler to understand that according to the law of the Spirit of life there never was any reality in sorrows and afflictions only such as we have imagined? It would be the nobility of one who understands the Science of God and chose to live it rather than one who kept on insisting that there is no Science of God.

"For this is Life eternal, that ye know the true God" (John 17:3). What does eternal Life mean? It

means that there is no end to any faculty. Seeing is an eternal faculty. To know the true God will keep the sight strong forever. Hearing is an eternal faculty. To know the true God will keep the hearing good forever. Self-providing is an eternal faculty. To know the true God will make us self-providing and self-sustaining forever.

This is what the first verse of this psalm means: *"The Lord is my Shepherd. I shall not want."* To know the law of God is to know the law of Spirit, for God is Spirit.

If one should sit right down in the midst of this sordid age and determine to get his provision from Spirit, and not by any material process whatsoever, would he be provided for? Yes. He would help to open the gates of the golden age, when no one can get anything away from anyone, and no one can get any power over any one. It ushers in the sight of Truth and we are ashamed of our batterings and calculatings. We can see that all ideas of buying and selling, giving and taking, borrowing and lending, had their rise in our covenantings with God to give us life, and health, and home, and heaven, if we could give Him faith, or praise, or penance. We should not attempt to barter with the true God for our blessings. *"He giveth to all men liberally"* (James 1:5). *'The gift of God is Eternal Life"* (Romans 6:23).

Eternal Life must be applied to our blessings as well as to our being. If you will not agree with your God to give Him anything or do anything for

Him, you will feel a thousand times more grateful when you see your safety and pleasure increasing day by day than if you should agree to praise, or acknowledge, or give thanks, for there is always a sneaking feeling of not having been half thankful enough or half conscious enough of the goodness of God if one has agreed to give thanks and praises for blessings received. And this sneaking feeling of not having half kept your obligations is very hardening to the character and irritating to the mind.

Many a man or woman is ugly or cross because he or she feels as if there were something they ought to have done which they haven't. And the hidden idea that you haven't half performed your obligations to your God, will end by your getting into debts which it will seem impossible for you to pay. Indebtedness to your fellow men is an awfully uncomfortable feeling. So in Science you are taught to go and make it right with your God and you will find it easy then to make it right with your neighbor. Tell the true God that you never owed Him anything and He never owed you anything. Speak boldly that as God cannot owe God, so you cannot owe God, for your substance, your life, your mind is God, and God is your substance, your life, and your mind.

Jesus taught this lesson of getting out of debt by a saying that has been translated this way: *"Forgive us our debts as we forgive our debtors"* (Matthew 6:12). Looking at the text from the scientific standpoint of David, as found in the sixth verse of this psalm, we see that "forgive us our debts" means give now into our mind Thy knowledge that there is no debt. As we now pass along the lines of Mind that there is no debt, we hereby drop our imagination that we could owe God anything, or that God could owe us anything. As God is the substance and life and mind of man, so man cannot owe man anything.

Will such reasoning make you careless about paying money you owe? No, it will provide you with easy abundance to pay what you have promised. It will "anoint your head with oil." It is the self-treatment farmers and working people should use. Talk to God that He owes you nothing and you owe Him nothing. There is no deal and barter in Spirit. There is no four and five are nine in Spirit. While anyone is hugging on to the idea of obligations to God, he will be constantly getting into some sort of obligations to his fellow man. The burden of his family becomes a disease. God provides abundantly. *"Goodness and mercy shall follow us all the days of our life."*

When you see the wolfish faces of the anarchists, nihilists, communists, pass the Divine Truth along to them that they owe no one and no one owes them, for God cannot owe God. Their thwarted hearts were first crushed under the heel of the religious teaching that penance was due God, faith was due Him, praise had not been half rendered, acknowledgment had been a failure on their part.

There is a loving truth shining up from one line in this psalm that makes me think of the way a diamond throws its sunshine from its angles and facets. It touches a dark corner of your mind with glory, precious child, if you look at it steadfastly. You cannot look at one of these texts, or even at a single word, but that finally it will shine with a loving meaning; but this one about *"dwelling in the house of the Lord forever"* is greatly bright for that hidden chamber in your heart, where the curtains are drawn so close that you will not admit to yourself that there is such a chamber, you keep it so dark. Let this light shine into it with me while we hold the candle of Science in our hand.

✷ It is that chamber where you keep the silent thought, "I made a great mistake; I wish I had not done and said what I did." The outcome of having such a dark chamber in your heart is vicissitude of fortune and friendship. Let us deal with it scientifically. There is no advantage in vicissitude. Religious people may tell you there is, but Science shows you plainly that there is not. To *"dwell in the house of the Lord forever"* means to dwell in that state of mind that keeps you prosperous and happy and beloved always. You cannot be prosperous, or happy, or beloved steadfastly while you have a place within you that repeats within itself, "I made a mistake, I made a mistake."

As God cannot make a mistake, so you could not make a mistake. There are no mistakes. "But," you say, "I did make the mistake and now I am desolate and unhappy in consequence." You do not need to speak from that standpoint just now. Speak from the spiritual standpoint a few minutes. You have spoken, and thought, and acted from the standpoint of having made a mistake, lo, these many years, and now it is only fair that you should speak from the standpoint of this text, which is Absolute Truth, for the few minutes we are together.

In Spirit which is your true nature, you are utterly incapable of making mistakes. In Spirit you are God. Ignoring the shadow nature with its dark claims, speak now with Truth from your spiritual nature saying, "I never made any mistakes; therefore I never took the consequences of any mistake. I am free." You had better speak often and much from your spiritual nature. Its name is, "I am," or its name simply is, "I." Let that "I" tell its tale of goodness and peace over and over till the old "I" with its tales of woe is never heard speaking or felt thinking any more at all. This "I" of you that never made any mistakes is Jesus Christ in you.

Jesus Christ is dominion and light and joy. How much of your time have you spent speaking from your spiritual nature? Pass your knowledge along over the airs to the unfortunate. They will stop speaking from that "I" of themselves which is so miserably sorry it made such mistakes in the past.

Job caught sight of the "I" that is not wicked, and though his best friends urged him to acknowledge his mistake, he declared he had never made any. So he came off victorious and unscathed. You must not let that nature speak now for you which says, "But it cannot be made up to me, now that the friends are gone and the home is broken up forever." In Truth, they were never taken away. By Truth, you are able to understand that it is all to you "as a dream when one awaketh." You must spend your time with Truth and see what it will bring. If you have never tried this way, of course you are not competent to shake your head unbelievingly.

There are many witnesses to testify to the satisfaction of speaking from the spiritual standpoint instead of from the material standpoint. Material experiences are ceasing to a great many people. They used to be careful and troubled about many things and they had to work fearfully. Today they are relieved of care and trouble and they do right works easily. They are living witnesses of the promise, *"My Presence shall go with thee and I will give thee rest"* (Matthew 11:28).

There are many tired mothers to whom you may pass the Truth that they are Spirit and not matter. Their pale faces will brighten when to the Divine in them that tries to speak and waits to be spoken to, you proclaim, "You are Spirit, and Spirit is free." As the ocean breeze refreshes the heat burdened traveler, so your breath renews the roses and the smiles of the youth of the motherhood on earth. To the friendless, you may be friend though you never speak to them or meet them. They are thinking perpetually from the standpoint of loss. In Spirit, nothing is lost or wasted. That which is in God goes to God. There is no loss. There is no loss even of your simplest possessions. There is no waste even in your kitchen.

Sit down by the river of that Truth and speak from the Spirit entirely for as long as you can. "There is nothing lost in Spirit. There is nothing wasted in Spirit. There is nothing lacking in Spirit."

As you preach this mysterious gospel in the silence of your mind, you will be told exactly where and how to restore unto yourself that which you seemed to have lost. Even your possessions that have seemed lost or wasted will come into your sight, and you may take them into your ownership again.

And speaking from this standpoint, your friends and your possessions will take on a new light. At first the result of saying that there are no mistakes or losses may not seem to be restorations. Some breakings-up may begin, breakings-up of the present states of affairs as they look. Even your present friends may change in the seeming. But your true words going forth from the Spirit will stand to the setting up in right order of all things.

Restoration is sure. *"I will restore unto thee all the years that the caterpillar hath wasted"* (Joel 2:25). Caterpillar means the speaking from the material standpoint. It makes you so hungry all the time, gnawing and wishing and longing and waiting. The "I" that restores and satisfies like a shepherd, is the Spiritual speaking, letting the Spirit tell its tales in your mind.

Pretty soon all the Science of God will be clear to you. Then you will be as bold as the rest in proclaiming that all study of material things is vanity, while the study of Spirit is the very power of God in you "all the days of your eternal Life."

April 24, 1892

LESSON V

EXTERNAL OR MYSTIC

Psalm 51:1-13

The fifty-first Psalm is both external and mystic. We will heed its mystic sense. In Science we learn that to study the external is to be baffled at every turn, — to finally end by the well-known saying of the physicists: "The most that we know is that we know nothing." We are always like that we are studying. The conclusions of the materialists are right. He has been studying nothing when he has been studying matter, and so he must know nothing. In Science we learn that to study the mystic or spiritual sense of all things is to glow and brighten with substantial understanding. For the mystic or spiritual is the real. To study the real is to show forth reality. This fifty-first Psalm is called the prayer of the penitent. It is David's misery because he has so speedily found out that he had believed falsely when he believed that adultery and murder would satisfy his heart.

All penitence has been discovered to be simply the howlings of those who are disappointed because mistakes have not made them happy. Some harden their hearts in anger. Some feel penitent

Penitence is a quicker road back to a chance to begin over again than hard-heartedness. But everyone goes back to his chance to begin over again somehow. There are none lost. They may sleep profoundly in hard-heartedness, and so be longer going back in mind to their first estate than the penitent, but they will wake up somewhere, somehow, sometime.

"Blot out my transgressions" cries David. This means make them nothing. "Against Thee, Thee only, have I sinned." As one cannot sin against Omnipotence, this was the noblest self-treatment David could have spoken. Omnipotence is the only power. There is, therefore, no power in sin. Omnipotence is the only Being. There is, therefore, no being to sin against the only Being. There is, therefore, no place, or space, or where, that sin could be committed.

Does this seem to be true reasoning when we look out upon the phenomenal world? O, no! It is pronounced in the highest sense ridiculous. Why, then, do we reason along lines that bring down so much derision and contempt? Because they are the lines that bring freedom from what seems to be sin. Because they are the lines that bring freedom from sickness and misfortune. The moment one declares that his sin or his crime is against

Omnipresence and Omnipotence only, he feels inwardly that it is blotted out from that moment. He is touching heart to heart with Spirit. He pays no attention to material men and women. He is a mystic and is happy. The first taste of the bliss of the mystic makes a difference in the actions of the individual. If you get this taste by clear, careful reasonings, you will be able to explain the way, and others may reason exactly as you do and taste the bliss and change their actions. If you stumble upon the taste, you may not be so good at explaining the process by which you were made so happy. Take these cases to illustrate. They explain the real meaning of the text, "Cast all your care on God." One woman was left a widow with a family of little children. She sat down with her babies around her and said positively that God must provide for her and her children. She held firmly on to this position in mind, and though her neighbors called her shiftless, she would not yield this point. They pointed out women who had opened boarding houses and shops. She held her ground. They told her that "God helps them that help themselves." All to no avail. She could not explain that she was taking literally the deepest meaning of the words of Jesus Christ, "Cast all your care on God."

She took the word "all" to mean all. And it turned out wonderfully. From the most unexpected quarters, beautiful gifts and bountiful provisions came to her. The neighbors said it was lucky that so shiftless a woman was so lucky in having presents which she had not earned. According to the Science of Jesus Christ, she had earned them in the only way that is legitimate. It is not scientific to order your life by the proverb, "God helps them that help themselves." It is not true. It is absolutely true that God helps them that let Him do everything. There was a beautiful church lately built by men who believe that "God helps them that help themselves." Every man who contracted to do any part of the building lost money, from the digging in the earth to the tipping of the spire. It was a wrong principle of action, you see. It was not easy for the woman to explain her feeling of "rest in the Lord to bring it to pass." It is easy for those who study the second Series of lessons in Spiritual Science to see and to put into practice, that God is the only provider, the only care-taker, the only worker. God is All.

David was mourning about his having thought he should be happy if he committed two crimes. By mourning over them and talking to God about them, he suddenly struck the treatment that will unburden anyone of the greatest sort or kind of mental weight. He looked right straight to God. He laid it all upon God. He that moment felt how utterly no where is sin, suffering, death, because God is all.

"Is there any besides Me?" saith the Lord. *"Do not I fill heaven and earth?"* The millions of unemployed laborers are here today the visible result of the religious teaching that the Lord helps those

who help themselves. The planet is convulsing with the conflicts of labor and capital because of that proverb. Their ancestors worked like galley slaves, and from their tired energies put forth these offspring. Our rich men work like galley slaves, and from their harassed forces put forth their incompetent offspring who will be the unemployed grumblers of the next generation. This is the process of generation according to the flesh. David says it is the being "shapen in iniquity." Jesus Christ put his finger back to the error in the mind which says that because we came forth from the flesh we are full of trouble, therefore we must earn our bread by the sweat of our brow, and said, *"Call no man upon earth your father for one is your Father, even God"* (Matthew 23:9). Then he erased the idea of laboring for your living with the words, *"Labor not for the meat that perisheth"* (John 6:27).

It would be a divine treatment of yourself if you would stop this moment and take Jesus Christ at His word by proclaiming mentally, "I never came forth from the flesh of the material world. I came forth from God. God is my Father and my Mother. I do not have to be anxious or careful about my living. God is my provider. I do not have to labor. God works for me. I do not believe in anyone's laboring for the meat that perisheth. I believe that God will clothe and feed all the world without their struggling any more than the lily struggles. From this moment I believe that God does all and everything. Amen." You must take all the texts of Scripture and push them to their extremest meanings. No matter how many fences have been put up by theology, so-called, be bold and reckless in taking inspirations of Spirit to be practically true.

David speaks of being restored unto the joy of salvation after he has mourned at his mother's having been a material woman. By a sudden gleam he found that he had been a child of God from the first. It is easy to erase the idea of material parents and wake up in "God our home."

We erase ideas from our minds by words. *"Let us take with us words and go unto our God"* (Hosea 14:2). It is a bath in the waters of Paradise to wash our old ideas of these Scriptures out of mind and take the texts just as they mean.

This planet has been called by poets and geniuses, "The sorrowful star." It has also been called the planet of doubt. It was found to be the only star whose inhabitants doubted the goodness of God. It is certainly a globe where it is written plainly that it is what we believe in our hearts that we show out in our lives.

We believe in heredity in the flesh and we show out that belief in inherited foolishness and inherited disease. We take Jesus Christ at His word and deny heredity in flesh and proclaim our heredity from God. As soon as the new idea gets any hold on our faith, we show healthy bodies and wise minds. There was an African king who believed that poisons were good to eat. He got to eating poisons all the time and flourished on them. Those who came near him did not believe that poisons were good to eat, so when he embraced them much, they died. His faith was death to his neighbors because it was not based in the principle that God is the life of the plants and the life of the world. He just believed in poisons as good for himself.

There is a man who has thought about force so much that he believes in force more than anyone in this country. This confidence in force makes him able to set immense masses of machinery into action. Another believes so intently in curing drunkards that he cures them at once. Both these men have limited the range of their ministry, though they do wonders as far as they go with their faith. You must have the faith of God, every one of you. You must eat Omnipotence. You will never be satisfied with anything less than Omnipotence. It will not take away from your neighbor's Omnipotence if you have eaten Omnipotence, any more than it could take away from your teacher's knowledge of Euclid if you should know as much as he does.

You must have all the riches of God, every one of you. Nothing will satisfy you short of all there is in creation. It will not take away from your neighbor's riches if you have all the riches there are in creation any more than it would take away from your neighbor's health for you to be healthy.

This is the "glory you had with the Father before the world was." David puts it here in the word "restore." Such a faith as this emanating from you will heal and uplift and feed the world. To believe any less than this is to show out less than perfect healing power, perfect helping energy, perfect judgment

It is believing less than we have a right to believe that makes us a sorrowful star and a doubter of the goodness and impartiality of God. "Uphold me with a free spirit," sings David. Last week the lesson was that men are anarchists because they are the product of the idea that we must pledge ourselves to give something to the Almighty if He will answer our prayers. We found the interior meaning to be that no one should ever pledge himself to do anything or to give anything or owe anything to God Almighty, but should agree with Him to do everything Himself, and give everything Himself for nothing, just as it is written, *"He giveth to all men liberally"* (James 1:5) and never scolds nor complains nor lays it up against anyone if she or he has not done penance nor given alms. This week the idea that reigns is the free Spirit. We see that there is no limit to our possessions and powers, every one of us, without interfering at all with our neighbor's possessions and powers. We find that it sets all minds free from the idea of earning bread by the sweat of the brow.

We find that the belief in earning wages of our fellow men is the curse, or the serpent upon whose head the woman shall set her heel in the last days of the material earth.

The Science of God is the woman. The belief in earning our living by the favor of our neighbors is the serpent of belief in some of our neighbors being wiser or richer or stronger than we.

Upon this idea that has wound its smothering coils around the earth the Science sets its heel of denial. No! There is no respect of persons with God. Each one owns all of God, and none can take from his neighbor's all. Each one knows all of God, and none shall be able to teach his neighbor, *"Lo, here is God, or lo, there"* (Matthew 24:23), for all proclaim they know Him, from the least unto the greatest. None shall earn his rights from his neighbor, but each shall receive without labor the gift of God. *"Labor not for the meat that perisheth"* (John 6:27). God shall uphold us with His free Spirit forever. "We trust in God." Such a doctrine as this held in the mind will fruit practically in new avenues of subsistence being opened up to those who by long belief in superiority and inferiority and earning from neighbors, are now our restless unemployed and our angry employed. There are metaphysical powers, quickening now within them as the Science of God wings her omnipotent way from God around them to God within them.

The stirs and throes that the planet feels are the working of the words of the free Spirit of the Science of God proclaimed from the earnest hearts

EXTERNAL OR MYSTIC   *Fourth Series*

of the fearless and true as they sit in the silence helping on the salvation from doubt and discouragement and inequalities that have no right in this Kingdom now coming into our sight.

May 1, 1892

LESSON VI

VALUE OF EARLY BELIEFS

Psalm 72:1-9

"With those elect,
Who seem not to compete or strive,
Yet with the foremost still arrive,
Prevailing still.
Spirits with whom the stars connive
To work their will."

There are some people who are bound to be foremost. "There's a destiny that shapes their ends, rough hew them how they will." They do not answer when they are accused.

They do not need to. They do not try to have their names enrolled on the scrolls of earth's great ones. They do not have to try. It is written in their foreheads that the nations shall call them blessed while they smile as little babies in their cradles. They are the answers to the prayers of the saints. Their minds are docile, simple, innocent, confiding, always. All children expect to be good. They look only for goodness when they stretch up their fingers and open their eyes for the first time in our arms. They expect justice. They take Providence for granted. And some little ones are left so free that they keep to the last that open expectation of the universe always doing the right thing by them. These are enrolled on the annals of fame.

For the universe purposes only good to us all. To keep our windows and doors open and in it all rushes. Such minds are the right kind of vacuum. The gods love them and come in and sup with them freely. And this is all there is to greatness — taking the best for granted.

Everything you ever accomplished you have accomplished because you have from childhood kept one childish trait of taking for granted. Maybe you dragged along the weight of supposing you would have to scramble and struggle to carry it out, but that was a notion that did not frighten you out of your childish expectation of some one thing.

To be supremely good one must be supremely childlike, taking no notion of having to try to be anything along with his expectation of all things. It is the children that enter the Kingdom of God.

This lesson is a wonderful reminder that it is never too late to be little children all over again. We may become again as we were when we were first born — knowing neither good nor evil, docile the will of destiny.

"Conduct me, Zeus, and thou, O Destiny, where'er thou wilt."

Solomon took many, many goods for granted. He took not the idea of enduring chastity; so in this Psalm (72) where his own expectation of righteousness left off, he saw by prophecy that one would come who, by reason of expecting all things, holiness included should, no matter what happened, be King of kings and Lord of lords.

When Jeremiah is forbidden to call himself a child, it is meant that he should not be after the order of one who cringes and trembles with fears of evil. This is not the child who is Son of God, equal with God, but the shadow of him.

Solomon says that this type of character shall be a judge, saviour, a king, a peacemaker, a bountiful provider, a counselor, friend, an instructor. He shall teach mankind how to have all things without scrambling and struggling. Jesus Christ taught this. He promised an hundred-fold more human goods by His principle of expectation than by all the methods of action now in use. He said that the bounty of the Spirit of the universe would fall wonderfully over those who would take things for granted, and in the next sphere of experience we would be sure to drop the notion of death: *"An hundred-fold more in this life, and in the world to come everlasting life."* (Luke 18:30) In noticing the expectations of good which have characterized the great, we mark that they all took death for granted. This is not laid up against them, but it is promised that they shall not take that into the next sphere of experience.

Here it is remembered that the mind of the profound thinker who has received the gift of seership has ever declared that for the most of us on the earth there are seven spheres of experience through which we must walk. This earth is one of them. Those who hasten their experiences here may pass the others, which have pain and sorrow, swiftly, hardly touching them with the wings of light which our life here in righteousness has furnished us. Jesus Christ intimates that most of the people passing the next sphere still expect death as the portal through which to step on into the next beyond. But those who understand Him will not take that belief along, and will fly the spheres on wings of deathless life.

As no one has yet entirely practiced His principle of expecting provisions of all kinds straight from the Spirit of righteousness, we have an entirely new field of Science before us. Solomon sees that it will be natural for gold and silver to flow to that kind of scientist. And gold and silver shall be nothing to him any more than the applause of people or the air he breathes. He shall see that all things are provided by the Spirit. He shall see that all things are done by the Spirit. It shall never occur to him to say that he wrote his books by hard work. He shall not think that he conquered his enemies by kindness. He shall see that the

Spirit wrote his books and the Spirit furnished him his friends.

Dickens told the people that he had only one genius, and that was the genius for hard work. The pugilist thinks his strength is his muscle, but there is nothing of intelligence or strength but God. It is acknowledging that it is God, that causes the work to bless the world with its light.

Every child heard its name called when it was young. Some listened and knew that the Spirit meant something for themselves alone. Others forgot. You heard your name called. Do you remember the day? Go back in memory, and sit down into that state of mind again for a moment. So lovely is this Spirit that broods overhead that all the intervening days may be blotted out, and you may to riches. You do not have to shout, drive a sharp bargain, nor hold your own in a deal. The devil must not find any food of such idea in you.

Sheba is a figure of speech for greatness of character and position. You do not have to try to be great. You were born to greatness. If you think for a moment that someone is going to get the position over you, then indeed you must take down the shutter of that notion. It is a bar of "bringing up," or cultivated characteristic of such a solid flesh substance that the devil eateth a good morsel by keeping you in an inferior position when you feel fitted to a higher one. Take your greatness for granted. Do not fight and connive. You need not pay someone to help you into your seat. Do you not see how you are taught that it shall come to you with this state of mind?

Sheba is a figure of speech for noble reputation. You came forth into this sphere with the expectation of the perfume of a reputation for virtue and wisdom.

If you laid across the open window the fear of misrepresentation or injustice, what torments you would feel from the bitings of report. Jesus kept that bar of human feeling away. It was a flesh spot the devil found not in Him at all. He was so silent at calumny that the Shekinah (Divine Presence) comes strolling over the ages from the temple halls of His presence on Calvary.

Sheba always stands for the perfume of Holiness. Of Sheba, Herodotus says that the land exhaled an odor of marvelous sweetness. Diodorous tells that the wondrous perfume thereof extended far out to sea.

Strabo said that this perfume of the spices of Sheba made them so valuable that Sheba was the wealthiest spot on earth. The people made their furniture of gold. This riches of Sheba signifies that to expect people to speak well of you is a sure state of mind to be supported by. It is a forerunner of poverty if one is afraid someone is talking against him. Loss of some goods will follow on that idea.

"The isles" is a figurative expression for believers in your doctrine — converts. Never think for an instant that people will not believe in your highest teachings. You were born to inspire confidence. Never think you must trim your sails to curry favor "Speak the word boldly that is given you to utter." Put no bar on your lips. "But," says one, "suppose one feels like preaching communism, free love, etc." He does not feel like preaching anything that defrauds a single creature of a thing if he is of the Messiah's mind. <u>This Psalm gives the description of how the mind with which you came forth expecting all people to believe in your words was the mind to help the needy and helpless, not to rob them</u>. The Messiah spends no time robbing nor preaching of such. The highest truth is the highest defense, support, strength, peace. Better not put the idea of getting away from your neighbor that which you want, across your childhood expectation of good. That is an idea that makes the torment of anger and resentment, very excellent eating for that devil of impotent rage which tried Jesus and went away as hungry as a shad of the seas of nowhere.

On the top of the mountains there is a handful of corn that can shake the earth with plenty, writes Solomon. The top of the mountain is the highest doctrine of Self. The Self is the I. The only I there is, is the one God. *"I am God, and there is none beside"* (Isaiah 45:22). Some day you will find the central intelligence of your being proclaiming His name within you. This will be after you have become as expectant of good as an infant.

There will be no bars of flesh — no human dreads. "Truth is not cumbered by matter." This is the handful of corn that shall drop its increase till the whole earth shall be filled with the knowledge of God as the waters fill the seas.

When that Name speaks within you, at the summit of your being, you will do great works easily. The Name shall speak a doctrine forth, to which every knee shall bow. At this moment it is proclaiming in a voice the ears of flesh tell you they do not hear, "I can preach the truth through you; I can heal the sick for you; I can cast down evil by your presence; I can raise the dead where you walk."

The glory of God from whom the child came forth need not have any coverings of flesh suitable for the devil to eat. There need be no imagination of evil to torment the earth. With this knowledge the imagination of evil is put away. The knowledge of truth is the only knowledge worth while. See what experience your ideas of evil have brought you. Watch what experiences your knowledge of truth will bring you.

Your first estate was God. You may drop what you have heard unlike God and be a child again seeing God. Expecting good from every direction you shine forth glory over all your world. You are of "those elect...with whom the stars connive to work their will."

May 8, 1892

LESSON VII

TRUTH MAKES FREE

Psalm 84:1-12

The information held within the chalice of these texts has been as carelessly handled as were the priceless manuscripts by the monks in the Nitrian monasteries of Egypt. Has anyone been preaching to believing audiences from these Psalms that the curse of earning our bread by the sweat of our brow, by hiring out to our neighbors, may be entirely removed by the right word? Has anyone found himself glad to be told that reformatories and prisons are no use because they are founded on a belief that in God's house there is evil? In Truth there are no criminals. In Spirit there is no need of prisons and reformatories. Spirit and Truth are all. Shall we, then, close up our prisons and reformatories? Our first duty is to know the truth about them. *"Ye shall know the Truth, and the Truth shall make you free"* (John 8:32). It is not for you to touch the externals. You are to know what is true. This is your whole business in life. Knowledge of Truth is its own demonstration. All things are coming to the world by its knowledge of Truth.

The Truth is, it is useless to study about heart beats, nerve ganglia, bones, and blood, for there are no such things. They are but the shadows thrown down from the belief in matter. As matter is nothing at all, of course there is no use studying it.

Schools and schoolmasters are no use for they are founded on the belief in the absence of intelligence. Such a belief is utterly without foundation in Truth, for Intelligence is God never absent from any jot or tittle of His universe. God is not "the Great Absentee of the universe," as we have been believing heretofore. God is the only Presence. Any institution or performance founded upon any other proposition than that God is Omnipresence must fall to nothingness, because it is founded upon a lie.

All material things and all performances, workhouses, hospitals, sanitariums, are but the shadows cast down by believing in the absence of God from some spot or point or creature of His house. The belief is a false one, and as God is the only Mind in the universe of course the mind that believes in evil and matter is no mind at all. The knowledge of this mighty Truth will stop your career of effort at reforming your neighbors, because it will stop your thinking such lies about them. The instant you stop thinking lies you enter into the silence. Here, at the silence of thinking what is not true, is heaven. *"And there was silence in heaven for the space of half an hour"* (Revelations 8:1).

It is the silence of that half hour within your own mind that has left you to let your imagination run riot. Enter into the silence of heaven, and the next speech that you speak will be from the Kingdom of Heaven within you. This Psalm is about the House of God. It is the eighty-fourth Psalm. It leads us to the most upsetting ideas. Ideas that upset our most vital beliefs of the past. We are able to see that God is all, and that to know the Truth of God will open the gates of gold. We find that we must have nothing to do in our minds with funerals or prisons or schools. If we do not allow our minds to think of such things they will never come into our sight. They will never come into anyone's sight who refuses to think of them, basing his cessation of thought on the knowledge that God being all, there is no room in Truth for evil or matter or death. Jesus taught this lesson by saying, *"Let the dead bury their dead"* (Matthew 8:22). He meant, "Let those whose thoughts are running on such things handle the consequences of their own thoughts."

If a funeral or hospital or sickness comes into our sight it is prima facie evidence we have let our thoughts dwell on lies concerning God. It is considered a virtue by some people to build hospitals and schools for the carrying out of man's belief in the absence of God. It is no virtue. It is better to enter into the closet and be still to know God. God is Truth. Truth will redeem the nations from pain. Therefore speak Truth. Truth is peace. Therefore speak Truth.

This dwelling in the House of God which is dwelling in freedom is the redemption from two subtle lies that are hanging their curtains before the eyes of those who are estimated as being very pious and godly. One subtle lie is the doctrine of fatality, and the other subtle lie is the doctrine of limitation. There is no fate. There is absolute choice, absolute monarchy. They who know God are above destiny. They know that they never did or said or thought anything in the past which could make a "karma" or weave a net of consequences around them with any reality in it. God is their past. *"I am Alpha"* (Revelations 1:8). They look forward to no future of the consequences of thoughts or actions or words in Truth, for *"I am Omega"* (Revelations 1:8). They laugh at the stories written in their stars. They set auguries and omens to one side. They are not amenable to society or custom. They dictate to society and bring forth the customs of God to overthrow the customs of the world. They know that the idea contained in the teaching of fate is nonsense. God is our home. Do they believe in death? There is nothing to die. God cannot die. God is all. I do not believe that —

> *"On two days it steads not to run from thy grave;*
> *The appointed and the un-appointed day.*
> *On the first neither balm nor physician can save;*
> *Nor thee on the second the universe slay."*

It sounds well, but it is the sound of a dreamer who hides the silence of heaven, where there is no place to run from but God, and no place to run into but God. To know this lesson well is to bring the world to an end. What world? Why, the dream world, of course. As a dream when one awaketh, so shall thy belief in old age foil off, thou Son of Jehovah, equal in power, equal in possession, equal in knowledge with thy Father-Mother God.

Does God grow old?

As a dream when one awaketh, so shall poverty and want flee from thee, thou bride of the Maker of world. *"Thy Maker is thy husband"* (Isaiah 54:5). Shall God refuse to provide? Here is a teaching. For you to be greatest in the kingdom does not mean that you are greater than your fellow man, but that you are the greatest you can be. How great can you be? As great as you have courage to affirm. To be wisest in the Kingdom of Heaven does not mean that you are wiser than any others, but that you are the wisest you can be. How wise is that? As wise as you have the courage to affirm.

To be richest in the Kingdom of Heaven does not mean that you are richer than your neighbors, but that you are the richest you can be. How rich is that? As rich as you have courage to affirm.

Riches are as Godlike as wisdom, and power, and health. *"Oh, the depth and height of the riches of God"* (Romans 11:33). That is the reason the world in its dreaming scrambles so for riches. It remembers its home and its plenty. *"Remember Me."* To know this truth will keep you from thinking it a virtue to be earning your living by any service to your neighbors. To know this will keep you from speaking of knowledge less than your neighbors. To know this will keep you from thinking yourself poorer or richer than your neighbors. You will be quick to affirm at the gates of silence the highest Truth you can speak of yourself. And you will know enough to unite yourself in eternal unity with Omnipotent Spirit. You must unite by the statement of faith. Faith is the uniting Substance. "Faith is the Substance." "I believe that my God is now working with me and in me to make me Omnipresent, Omnipotent, Omniscient; I believe in Jesus Christ." Why do you say, "I believe in Jesus Christ?" Because Jesus Christ means demonstration of Truth. At the gateway of heaven stands Jesus Christ, *"I am the door. Ye believe in God, believe also in Me"*(John 10:9).

"God (in Science) out of Jesus Christ, is a consuming fire." That is, even the Science as we teach it chemicalizes with strange experiences, without the statement, "I believe in Jesus Christ." The denial of evil for instance, causes all manner of evil to come into your lot saying, "Do you mean that I am nothing? In me hunt your home. Can you prove me nothing now?" Here you are saved by meeting the results of your faith in demonstration. This is the mystery of Christ. It will not be clear until we have stood within its substance by faith. "I believe in God within me and without me. I believe in Jesus Christ." This faith is above limitations, *"All things are possible to them that believe"* (Mark 9:23). *"All power is given unto Me"* (Matthew 28:18). And unto the Jesus Christ faith or the Jesus Christ man is given dominion over everything, so that he can say to the mountain, *"Be thou removed"* (Matthew 21:21) and it must be done. His word is enough. The man who believes in Jesus Christ, which is believing in the visibility of God, builds his church on a different foundation than the idea of saving souls. He knows that there is only one Soul and that is God. Does God need saving? So he builds a church or temple within his mind — *"not made with hands"* (2 Corinthians 5:1). This temple is the lofty Truth concerning the universe and man. The loftiest idea he can name he does name. And the loftiest ideal he can form of God is that there is no one to save, for all are saved. This fills his heart with praise. This is the true temple. He builds his factories and shops on another foundation than the supposition that man must he clothed and fed and housed. He knows that there is but one man, and that is God. Does God need shoes and killed lambs? Does God need the labor of little children to beautify his home?

These things are the fruits of believing that there is someone besides God, and some place besides the Kingdom of God.

So in the mind the man of faith describes God as clothed in the Beauty of Holiness. And his description of God being true, his thoughts go spreading over the universe like angels' fingers to lift the babies out of the factories and the lambs and calves out of the clutches of the butchers.

"He has his feet shod with the preparation of the gospel" (Ephesians 6:15), this man does. This all transpires within his mind before the works are made manifest. This is the day when that angel sounds whose voice causes the elders to fall on their faces and the kingdoms of the world to become in visibility, as they are in Truth, the kingdoms of our Lord and His Christ.

The voices that speed through the air are from heaven. Listen to them, you who have eaten and drunk and been clothed with things which your heart would ache to remember whence they came to you. Clothed with God, mantled with thoughts. Fine and cheery with Truth. Fed with God. Living by the words that proceed from the Father. All this is the Truth. All else is but dreaming. These thoughts within your mind first are the finger of God writing on the walls of the universe the things that shall shortly come to pass. The looms must stop at the sound of the voice of this Truth. Do you hear the threats of the rebellious multitudes, with their red flags, their refusals to work, their strikes, their anger? They are the shadows cast by the beliefs of the dreamer who thinks thoughts that are not true.

They will not come to bloodshed. The angels of peace are speeding forth from the workshops of Truth in the mind and all that is good in them will be fed with a new kind of food. All that is false in them will fall under the sword of the Spirit.

A new kind of loom is weaving today. A new kind of grist is grinding today. A new army has arisen today. The silent host of God. The old things fade and fail. "Hark! the herald angels sing."

"Chanting the mighty evangel
That hastens the spirit to free.
'Tis liberty's beautiful angel
Coming straight from the Father to thee."

What a wonderful meaning this Psalm yields up. Did you ever think along with its Truth before? Notice how it spreads its wings of protection: "The Lord is a sun and a shield. He will give grace and glory. No good thing will He withhold."

We do not turn away from the visibility of this providing and protection of Jehovah. We believe in demonstration because we believe in Jesus Christ; the Truth and its practical application to the daily affairs and places of our lot. According to this the looms and the shops and the marts and the armies ought to stop. God hath ordained the end of things founded on imaginations. "But the gospel must be preached to all nations." It is first in all minds, and then in all actions. Take your mind off material things. Fix it on Truth: Spiritual Science is Truth.

May 15, 1892

LESSON VIII

FALSE IDEAS OF GOD

Psalm 103:1-22

According to spiritual law it is found that it is good for the health to get hold of some principle and stand by it. If one is changeable, variable, unreliable in his ideas, one day believing one thing and another day believing another, he will be changeable, variable, unreliable in health. If he looks at principles or teachings to find what is true to his way of feeling, he will certainly be changing his ideas often, because feelings are no criterion for basing judgment upon.

Feelings are dependent upon weather and victuals, upon finances and friendships. Then the writings of Schopenhauer or Emerson may strike the mood, and one is a pessimist or an optimist according to the book that hit his feelings. Many a physical infirmity might be traced to the reading of a book full of brilliantly expressed falsities, like: "There is no place where earthly sorrows are more felt than up in heaven; though it has pleased God to send upon me this great affliction of palsy."

Maybe the mind had been thinking of the Kingdom of Heaven as an abode of peace and rest. Maybe the mind had been believing that God is goodness, and has no substance in Himself out of which to make palsy; but here are these sentimentally expressed lies, and away go the ideas of God and heaven which would have been such a reliable tonic to the blood. This 103rd Psalm selected for the International Course has for its golden text, *"Bless the Lord, O my soul, and forget not all His benefits."*

It tells that it is possible to drop all our old notions, and thereby drop our old conditions any minute. It teaches that mistaken ideas are the cause of every bit of sickness, every bit of hunger, every bit of old age, every bit of cruelty, every bit of pain, every bit of misfortune. It reminds us it is easy to drop mistaken ideas and leave ourselves free from miseries of all kinds.

It teaches that to have the right idea of God is the first important state of mind to be conscious of. Whoever declares that he will not have anything at all to do in his mind with the idea of a God sending hardships of any kind has proclaimed a principle of thinking which will work wonders with him if he will not let appearances strike him down from his Principle.

Appearances and feelings must count against your Principle. The Principle will lay the appearances low when you have held by it long enough to believe it in your heart.

The marvel about this Psalm is, that it lays out the appearances of old age that so many people have, and shows it up as just the result of believing in a God of limited generosities. It comes of believing in a stingy God. A stingy God is one who gives His children eyesight for a limited time and then shuts off on it. A stingy God gives vigor and intelligence up to a certain point and then begins in a tantalizing manner to withdraw them. This Psalm is very explicit in declaring that if one has the true idea of God in his mind and won't be shaken off his basis for a moment that he shall *"renew his youth like the eagle."*

There is such a thing possible as getting the right idea of God and holding right to it until your youth returns, your strength renews, your beauty comes forth, your vigor rises, your health is perfect. Read over the Psalm and then follow these ideas, which it discloses to the bold mind of one who pays no attention to appearances, but fearlessly regards reasoning according to Jesus Christ as the right interpretation. The ministers that do the pleasure of God are those who accomplish His kind of works. *"If I do not the works of the Father, believe me not."* (John 10:37) But if by reason of this Principle anyone brings to pass its works in even a slight degree we will take up the Principle and hold by it till we also do like works, or even greater works inasmuch as we may have some larger appearances and stronger feelings to meet than he seems to have. Any system of religion that lets its ministers get old and toothless, gray and tottering, spectacled and poverty-stricken, is not the Truth of God no matter if those ministers can reel off Sanskrit by the cargo to confirm their ideas. All these conditions have got to go away off the planets under the ministry of Truth.

The fourteenth, fifteenth, and sixteenth verses describe man as he seems to us while we are looking through the spectacles of believing that God made him a mortal and fleshly thing instead of out of His own immortal Substance. Looking at mankind through such a mistaken idea of God's creative powers we see all performances of mortality that are so deplorable.

Turning our minds off those people and telling the Truth about God's creations, we withdraw our belief from mankind, and away go all those appearances that made us feel so badly. <u>Everything is glued together particle by particle by our believing.</u> <u>Withdraw the glue of our believing and they are gone</u>.

Beliefs in lies rot. They fail as glue fails. There is nothing in a lie anyway. It seems to have quite a hearing for a while but it is nothing. The man of flesh seems to be something for quite a while but the first thing you know he is gone. All flesh is the appearance of a lie. There was a way of thinking about that man which would have glorified his presence till there could not have been any departure from Him. All material or mortal and transitory appearances will vanish out of our sight when we do not believe that <u>God ever made anything to die or be limited in power or wisdom or length of life</u>.

Eternally increasing beauties and strengths and faculties stand forth upon our steadfast confidence in a truth.

Those who begin to name a truth that they wish to believe in and see come out in life often come to a stopping place because it seems as if their words about goodness did not work out any better conditions for them; but, if anything, matters went worse than ever with them. This is the time to be firmer than ever. It comes to the whole planet full of people if you send them word that <u>you do not believe there is any evil in them</u>. It comes to your affairs if you send them word that <u>you do not believe in failures</u>. It comes to that sick man to whom you have given the bath of withdrawing <u>the belief in his sickness</u>. They all show up worse than ever. This is Satan let loose for a thousand years. Who is Satan and what are a thousand years?

Satan is the subconscious belief in evil which you may be surprised to find you have kept hidden in your mind. The very hidden ideas of evil must stand out for you to withdraw your belief from. You must unglue every memory of evil from your mind. When all the nations are angry, just as it mentions in the book of Revelations, and Satan is let loose, it means that we have come face to face with all the smothering beliefs in evil which lie under our plausible conscious thinking about the goodness of God and His immortal and perfect creations. The most pious devotees have kept a mental reservation about the evils that might possibly come to them, even while they were singing praises of the goodness of God. <u>That was their satan in the hidden places</u>. By and by that reservation comes fronting us in whatever we have spoken about as Good. It will last in our sight till we bring up from the deepest region of our mind the efficient idea, <u>*"I do not believe in evil at all I believe in the Good only."*</u>

While this final determination is ungluing even our unconscious belief in the possibility of evil in God's universe, it is our thousand years. <u>The term 'thousand years' simply means period of final struggle.</u> "For the elect's sake those days shall be shortened." That is, we may be so determined to stand by our Principle that old errors give up their appearances at once. Determination is a terror to Satan. The words, "I do not believe in evil at all. I believe only in the Good," are the arrangement of a new base in mind and a new set of circumstances in life.

Every bit of the miracle working of Jesus Christ is easy to one who has established his base in Truth. Satan is to be bound and cast into the bottomless pit. That is, even our remotest reservations concerning the evils that might possibly come upon us are to be utterly annihilated.

And not only ours but the beliefs in evil that the world has held, will be utterly annihilated. Everything has to be done in mind first, before crimes and pains and misfortunes perish from the seeming. Thus the greatest ministry you can give forth is the ministry of your right thoughts. The greatest good you can do is to spread the gospel. You may fit out some missionaries to go telling this Principle. You may encourage some faithful minister of it whose bidding is to stand boldly out and give up his former ways of making a living for its sake. But believe it and preach it you must — some way, somehow. This will shorten the thousand-years symbol, or your struggle with your present environment, after seeing the reasonableness of this Science.

It is reasonable, is it not, that if it will make your stomach strong enough to digest any sort of food if you will tell yourself that you are strong enough to do anything you please and material food can not dictate to you, and if you can drink the strongest coffee and tea without their affecting you at all by the same assertion, that gin and rum and tobacco are as harmless as anything by the same line of reasoning? It is reasonable to you, is it not, that if schools are all founded on the idea of absence of intelligence, as soon as that idea of the absence of intelligence is withdrawn the schools will tumble down out of sight? Their foundations being taken out they must fall, mustn't they?

It is reasonable to you, is it not, that if the reformatories are built on the idea that the Good is absent from some spots or creatures of its own creating, they must all fall into nothingness when we know the Truth that there is no absence of Good? It is reasonable to you, is it not, that if Satan is the product of our belief that God has made an opposite to himself, there will be no Satan when we do not believe God made anything unlike Himself?

It is reasonable to you, is it not, that if God occupies all spaces and places, and as astral spooks and elementals are the product of our belief in spots of the universe where God is not the substance, these must all be seen as pure nothingness without any power to hurt, when we withdraw our belief of the absence of the Substance of God from some spots of His kingdom? It is reasonable to you, is it not, that if the mathematics of the schools are all founded on the supposition that five balls and five balls are ten balls, when there are no balls, the mathematics of the schools are all a farce? By studying the Science of God or Spirit we find that all numberings and calculations are but the symbols of eternal verities, and that we had better be studying the eternal verities than the symbols of them.

The geometry of God is the statement of an Absolute Truth as its starting point; the straight line of an irresistible reasoning; the triangle of the fulfillment of a word of good in the life; the square of the daily proclamation that Truth preaches its own gospel, heals the sick, casts out demons, raises the dead; the circle of the beautiful gift of clothes and food and shelter and home without working for them, either as rich slaves or poor servants; the sphere of understanding how to breathe the airs of heaven and see and hear only the good; the pyramid of triumphant forgetfulness of the former heaven and former earth, high over the memory of the dream of mortality with its beliefs in the wickedness and absence of God, with our name written in our foreheads, that Name which stands in Spirit for the special work set out for us to do in the kingdom from whence we came forth. To know our own name is the only knowledge that is worth while.

May 22, 1892

LESSON IX

BUT MEN MUST WORK

Daniel 1:8-21

Does not the Bible tell us that man is to labor for his living, earning his bread by the sweat of his brow?

It tells us that man <u>under the curse</u> earns his living by the sweat of his brow, but under the Gospel he is set free from that curse. He is under the Gospel to *"Labor not for the meat that perisheth"* (John 6:27). He is told that the seed of the woman shall bruise the curse. What is the seed of the woman? It is the teaching of Divine Science. The Science of Christ is figured by a "Woman" in John the Revelator's mind. When we are quoting Scripture, it will help us to know where we stand and what we are talking about if we will explain whether we are speaking of what goes on under the curse or under the Gospel.

Does it make any difference to our daily lot in life whether we are speaking of man under the curse or under the Gospel? Indeed it does. *"As a man thinketh in his heart so is he"* (Proverbs 23:7). Many a man or woman could trace all their misfortunes to their continual harping on the Adam and Eve side of life, describing the dire effects of the fall and curse side. They might have been joyous and powerful if they had let their mind rejoice in the knowledge that words of Truth can annihilate the curse ideas as soon as they show themselves. What made the curse? The law of opposition. The idea of the opposite of the Jesus Christ man. *God created only One man - the Jesus Christ man.*

Is it not beneficial to study the ways of the opposite of Jesus Christ? Just as beneficial as to study the shadows of trees and rocks. Is it not reformatory to keep statistics of crime and records of horrors and tell them often to public audiences? Just as reformatory as it would be to study discords and not harmonies in music. We become like what we study. In this lesson on Daniel in the court of Babylon are we not taught that poor food is more consistent with a righteous life than rich food? It teaches that there is just as much nourishment in one kind of food as another. Food is a symbol of religious thoughts. Daniel meant to intimate distinctly that he did not relish their religious ideas. At home in Jerusalem he had eaten meat and drunk wine. There those foods symbolized the reviving words of Truth and the strong will of God. Here in Babylon they stood for the great idols, Bel, Merodach, and Nebo, to whom

[margin note: Great sermon or article]

sacrifices were offered. They intimated that man is governed by stars and suns and moons. They declared man is the victim as to happiness and health of blind forces. Indeed, material science was the god of Chaldea then, just about as material science is the god of civilization today.

In the fourth verse of this chapter of Daniel you will see that Daniel, Hananiah, Mishael, and Azariah understood the Science of God or the Science of Spirit.

God is Spirit. Understanding this Science they were able to symbolize their ideas of the difference between material science and Spiritual Science by eating a totally opposite kind of food from that eaten by their captors. They compelled pulse and water to signify the difference of their religion from the Babylonians. Was it necessary for them to signify their different ideas by different eating? No, But in those days everything was signified by symbols. Every idea had its outward action rigidly observed, as the Jews used the water of jealousy, the water of separation, water of feasts, etc., symbolically. Their teachers spoke in symbols. The first chapter of Genesis is symbolic. The second chapter of Genesis is symbolic. One stands for the Science of Spirit and the other for the science of matter. Whoever studies the first chapter will understand Substance, Truth; whoever studies the second chapter will understand nothing. Whoever thinks both chapters refer to man in reality will become much mixed. Whoever knows the first chapter well can handle the second one understandingly. Evidently Daniel understood the first chapter thoroughly, because he could make pulse and water do him as much service as meat and bread. Would he not have made a nobler demonstration of his spiritual understanding if he had gone three years without eating anything at all? Going without eating would have been to his mind a symbol of having no religion at all. It would have been the same symbol to his captors also.

Would it be a good plan for us nowadays to regard our eating and drinking as symbolizing the words and will of God? It is true that eating and drinking indicate the state of our mind religiously. If we feel hungry we can be sure that there is some word concerning the will and purpose of our God which our mind longs for. If we eat even to gorging ourselves we shall wish we could keep on eating till the knowledge of that will comes to us. If we drink we shall keep on drinking and wish we could drink more, even longing and thirsting for drink till we imbue drinks with strength to intoxicate, while the mind longs for some good news from Truth. Whoever is thirsty for strong drinks is wild for strong words of Truth. Where shall we get those strong words of Truth? We shall find them in Spiritual Science. At present Spiritual Science uses words just as much in the symbol as Daniel used eating and drinking, but there are certain signs now of Spiritual Science words bringing forth the full power of their substance right soon.

All Spiritual Science words so far have been like alabaster boxes. They contain precious ointments but the alabaster boxes have not been broken. What do you mean by breaking open words as you would break open boxes?

I mean receiving the quality of their meanings. How can you tell when they are broken open and the words have poured out their ointments? When the words concerning God as our health have made us every whit whole, so that there is no blemish in us as there was no blemish in those four young Jews. When the words concerning God as our support have given us assurance of abundant provisions right in our sight and manageable with our fingers, just as all things were given to those four young Jews who lived by Spiritual Science in the midst of an age that lived by material science.

In this age of material science the Spiritual Scientist should be defended by the supernal beings who fought for Elisha (that most perfect Spiritual Scientist of old). The Spiritual Scientist should be fed and clothed by the angels who ministered to Jesus Christ. When he breaks open the alabaster boxes of these mysterious words he is now using he will find that the end of the world has come and the beginning of his life has sprung forth. Who were those supernal beings around Elisha? They were his thoughts personified. If he had seen demons and devils they would have shown the quality of his thoughts. But, as he had

<u>no such thoughts no such being appeared to him</u>. The angels that ministered to Jesus were His supernal ideas. The more lofty our ideas the more defense and support there is in them.

How shall we break open these words we are now using? <u>By speaking them fearlessly</u> as the faith of our life. <u>By writing them down carefully</u> as the light of our judgment, by which we would be judged. <u>By thinking them silently as the only thoughts worth thinking</u>.

Ought a man sit down and fold his hands while his children go hungry that he may meditate on spiritual doctrines, seeing that all labor is the sign of living under the curse? No. He must keep swinging his hammer and balancing accounts till his knowledge of Truth takes those tasks out of his hands.

Spiritual knowledge itself does the turning and over-turning. It is very subtle in its workings. It is so secretive that the eyes and ears take no cognizance of it. But by and by its mission is visible. Knowledge of Truth is irresistible action.

At Kenilworth we saw, "on the rains of solid masonry in one place the swelling root of a creeper had lifted one arch from its base, and the protruding branches of a chance spring tree had unseated the keystone of the next," wrote a traveler. Just so all these evidences of civilization shall be subtly undermined, even to the stoppage of steam-cars and sewing machines, by the words of Jesus Christ concerning eating and drinking and shelter. Was not Jesus Christ poor so that He had not where to lay His head? No; He owned all the kingdoms of the world and the riches of them. When He wanted to fit out His disciples with purses and swords He did not have to work and earn them, He simply had to speak the word and it was done.

What did He mean by saying that the foxes had holes and the birds of the air had nests but the Son of Man had not where to lay His head? He was speaking of that man who had imagined he wanted to follow His doctrine when he had not the faintest idea of what it was. The Son of Man is the word of God. The man had not let anything but the teachings of the schools and the business of the stores and factories rest in his mind. Not a single idea that there is a way of living untouchable by deal and barter, work and study, had ever rested in his mind.

Daniel and his three friends lived by a Principle that was their defense and support, and yet they did nothing like the Babylonians. This Principle of living is now being proclaimed. One after another of its adherents is being removed from the ways and works of the world. The end of material things has touched the hem of their garments. Will this doctrine hasten the end of the world? Yes. The end of looking to material things and being hurt by the world's forces comes with speaking Truth. Will there be terrible times upon the earth? The end of a shadow at high noon is peaceful; so the end of materiality as represented by civilization cometh as a thief in the night, softly. There is no shadow at high noon. There is no materiality under the reign of Spirit. At high noon you may speak some great affirmation, and you will never see any shadow to it. Twelve o'clock is high noon time. Exactly at twelve every day tell God what you would like to demonstrate better than anything else. Then affirm it as already done. In reality it is already done, so you only speak a great truth when you affirm that a good thing is finished. To someone whose heart was depressed by misfortune these words were given as so bright that no misfortune could evermore lurk near her lot. She must keep them at twelve: "I am satisfied with my abundant prosperity, which from this date makes no delay in pleasing me."

To another whose heart was clogged with earthly cares the direction was given: "Write a letter to Jesus Christ and state your case exactly. Ask for help. Burn the letter and tell no one." You can focus all your mind and soul and heart into a letter. Writing is a great mystery. Jesus Christ wrote in the sand. Both these ideas come from the misty past of the mystics like Daniel and his friends. They disdained nothing and observed everything, even to interpreting dreams. They knew the law of high noon and morning and evening prayers. They did not need the second chapter of Genesis, which is the Babylonian side of the interpretation of symbols, which is judging man as on the down grade or curse side, a fallen creature under the curse of dependence upon skill and material things. No. They regarded all things as signs and symbols of our opportunities to step out of the shadow, away from Adam, out and away from the ways of materiality.

We will use nothing henceforth as signs of the needs of mortal and material man, but all things as signs of the opportunity of spiritual man to proclaim his exemption from matter and evil and the laws thereof.

This manner of looking at things will post you in languages without studying them. It will give you skill in mathematics without investigating them. It will give you the history of the sun and explain for you the times and seasons of constellations and comets.

Read this first chapter of Daniel with the knowledge that Chaldean science is all science of materiality, from astrals down to marble quarries. Take it home as a demonstrable verity that the understanding of Spirit gives easy mastery of all these things. If you do not catch this lesson you will not rise up in your greatness, but plod along in your present appearance. Yet there is a Spirit in you all, and the inspiration of Omnipotence giveth understanding of Spirit.

May 29, 1892

LESSON X

ARTIFICIAL HELPS

Daniel 2:36-49, Revelations 12: 7, 8

Confucius observed that there is a common faculty possessed by all men in equal shares, which if cultivated makes the serf the peer of the prince, the unbooked the peer of the savant. A certain sea captain noticed that on the Island of Madagascar and among the natives on the coasts where his ship put in at Africa and Australia there was the use of another sense practiced besides the senses ordinarily exercised. By the use of this faculty or sense they could foretell storms and calms, fair weather and foul with far greater accuracy than our weather bureaus are able to do.

Their system was quick and simple. It was as open as nature's sweet face. Ours seems to be stilted and complex. Ours seems like studying shadows. Theirs seems like converse with the Substance that casts the shadows. There were other things the seers among the "heathen" could tell besides weather. They could foretell earthquakes and tidal waves. They could see the march of human events ahead. They could read the signals of the stars. There was one item in common with civilization, however; they could not prevent tidal waves, nor annul coming disasters. They rendered up a verdict exactly like Job's, *"The thing I feared came upon me"* (Job 3:25). This is a civilization's proudest summing up: "Mankind is under the evangel of despair; we are all on a train bound for destruction. The most that we know is that we know nothing."

It was upon such times that Daniel appeared in the courts of Babylon. All the learning of the world was gathered under Chaldean skies. Their mathematics and music, their astronomy and surgery, business methods and commerce, were as dry and dehumanizing as ours of today. One of our profoundly learned physicists writes lamentingly, "There is a wide-spread want of an enlightened spiritual philosophy that shall counteract the materializing tendencies of the study of the natural sciences, which attribute faculties and functions to blind agents and give material forces and combinations the power to control life and destiny."

With his measure of the simple Judean spirit, unmixed with the stilted sciences of the highest civilization of that day, Daniel reproduced the dream of Nebuchadnezzar. In no way did Daniel suggest putting the coming kingdoms on their guard to strengthen themselves and prevent their demolition. He read their coming doom without the proposition of a remedy.

If he saw that the coming kingdom triumphant was to be the kingdom of spiritual morals he did not say so. If the king of material monarchies appreciated that the algebra and mathematics of ethical law should supersede the pride of worldly sciences he gave no sign.

Those figures stand out on the canvas full of information as the Sphinx's face.

In the realm of religion there are the golden, the silver, the brass, the iron and the clay periods. In the realm of science the same characteristics are apparent. In the realm of political movements, from gold to clay is history.

It is the common conviction that the days we are not experiencing are the last of materiality. *"The stone cut out without hands is smiling the image of all the ages"* (Daniel 2:44); and breaking the religious systems, the scientific calculations, the governmental policies, in pieces.

"The kingdom on the earth, though not of it" (John 18:36) is begun. The sound of its unseen hammer is the restlessness of nations, the conflict of capital and labor, the dragging forth into the sight of "the iron and clay mixed" science and religion and government, of the "Ishmaelites of Civilization" (see June issue *Arena Magazine*) the rise of woman, the disgust of the observing of our

school system, the general dissatisfaction at the existing order of things.

Whosoever preaches must preach that the old dispensation has closed. We will have none of it. He must preach that the new dispensation has begun. "Its will be done." This is the time when Michael and his angels fight against the dragon and his angels, and the dragon and his angels fight among themselves, but not against Michael and his angels, for they cannot see them.

The conflict of human dynasties is among themselves. The name Michael signifies there is only God. The angels with Michael are the teachings that belong to that proposition. The dragon is the belief of mankind that there is another power besides God, another substance besides God, other laws than God's laws. The angels with the dragon are the necessary ideas that go with such a great error of belief. These angels or ideas, with the people that represent them, get into a final fight among themselves. Each system blames the other for the universal restlessness, but no man blames his neighbor for the dissatisfaction that stirs his breast. Let him listen at the gates of silence. It is Michael and his angels moving down on the wings of the hour with the Supreme Truth — there is only God.

The conflict is first in the mind. Then it shows forth in the nations. Art, with its images of sense suggestions, falls down. Religion, with its proclamations of evil, crumbles. Science, with its artificial helps to life and health, falters and fades as the shadows of a ghost dance. Governments hang their heads and go out under the reign of demented, senile, or profligate rulers. They all are the outward formulations of the mental convictions of a power and a substance and a ruling besides God, the never absent good. However pious you have been, have you not believed in the necessity for evil, the reality of evil, the possibility of evil? That was your reserved opinion, was it not, while you were praising Jehovah and His Jesus Christ? Even at the golden height of your noblest consistency of conduct with belief, was such a reservation right? That reserved opinion has been the harboring of the dragon within your mind. If you have mixed it with the systems of church, or state or society of today, you are in at the "clay and iron age," and the blows of the silent doctrine cut out of the rock of Revelation are being felt by you in your restlessness and dread of coming evil.

The stone cut out of the universal rock is the bold word that there is only good intended for us all. Those two great doctrines in the mind have now come face to face. Those who recognize the reasonableness of the message of the archangel proclaim that *"there shall no ill come nigh their dwelling"* (Psalms 91:10).

They smile at the host of Michael and answer back while the shakings of empires signal the end of all flesh, that *"all things work together for good to them that love God"* (Romans 8:28), and they love the good God who sendeth only good.

With the acceptance of this proclamation that there is only good intended for us, there is no standing helpless at the sound of the earthquake. There is no expectation of death. Even the body knows that its mission is to transform and transfigure and not to be buried and fall into ashes.

The intellect hears the trump of Love sounding in the crash of governments, and takes on the glance of Omnipotence when it receives the doctrine cut out of the rock without hands of mortality. This doctrine is that "God is all; there is only God." Nothing that opposes can stand under the fall of its hammers. No argument based on history or science, or experience, or appearances of any kind can do anything but rise like a baffled worm of nothingness to assert its vanity and die away in the shame of absence. When this trump sounds *"they shall not judge after the sight of the eyes nor the hearing of the ears"* (Isaiah 11:3), for they shall know that all those things seen by eyes and heard by ears are the embodiment of the headstrong belief in mind that there is another presence besides God, another power besides God, another kingdom besides God's. They shall realize that any faculty that is still of the clay of imagination, whether it be the keen sense of the Madagascar child of nature or the stilted computations of civilized science. Though one should rise from the grave where you laid him in tenderness and from the sphere of the cloudy substance of astrals should foretell doom you would give him the lie, for you would know he was still of the clay of imagination, while the Truth is God has only good for you and no evil or pain or fear forever.

All things that shake and tremble are founded on the belief of another power or presence or law besides God. They are an image of nothing — an imagination without substance. They are the opposite of Truth. Side with them and evaporate like mist. Side with Truth and live in fullness of joy.

When you rise in the morning, are you afraid of the day? It is the dragon and his angels who fear. It is imagination that trembles. The trump of Gabriel, the hammer of the new kingdom, the war cry of Michael is calling you to make your choice of truth or error; of "God is with me," or "not with me." Every day sounds its toxin: Choose! Every item of the day gives you the chance to proclaim what manner of faith you are of. Do you believe that God guides all your steps in safety and your affairs successfully, or do you not? When you purposed to bring to pass that particular result and each item thwarted you, as it seemed, did you see that that which was being thwarted was of the clay of imagination? Did you fret and be anxious, or rejoice in the sight of the workings of Good?

In the stillness of your own chamber alone, do you appreciate that your millions are clay if one man can say, or one woman, or one child, that you overreached them? Do you know what that trembling signifies, which seizes your limbs sometimes, or gives you the blues? It is the dragon of imagination calling for his own destruction. It is the hammer of the Spirit striking its blows on your old ideas. Do not hesitate an instant. Proclaim, "I surrender my religion, my business policy, my possessions, to God."

Then there shall walk by you a High Counselor, a noble comrade, a powerful friend. You will not then need to be careful and anxious lest someone get away from you what belongs to you. God is the pleader of your cause,

The light of His countenance shall shine on those with whom you have dealings, and they will be kind and true. Their Spirit shall respond to the Spirit that walketh by you and they cannot do you wrong. Every attempt at it will meet with defeat. *"No weapon that is formed against thee shall prosper"* (Isaiah 54:17).

This is the second chapter of Daniel. It is the counterpart of the twelfth of Revelation, seventh and eighth verses. It is the proclamation of the highest Truth in all the brightness of its glory. It tells that though science and religion, and government have been as gold, at their best on this planet, their reign was imagination, for they have reasoned on the necessity for evil and the reality of material things. At their best they have calculated on the basis of two, when there is only one. So religion has come to her clay and iron age and at her best she cringes and flinches under the storms of this age, proclaiming with her latest breath that "God in His wisdom has suffered these things to be." It is a lie! God never permitted or ordained evil. It is all imagination. Let now the failure of the idea of two purposes in the mind that is God be our instruction. Science also has reached the formation of her understanding and looks helplessly upon the conflicts of poverty and riches, learning and ignorance. She has studied matter, when Spirit was her province. She sees no safety from cyclones, no help out of floods, no prevention of accidents. Governments have now struck the mire of their first imaginations, viz., that there are some who shall sit in judgment and reign over their neighbors, when the Truth is, all are one. There is no one to govern. God is the only Being and needs no dominion over Him by any other creature.

His word is, *"There is none beside Me"* (Isaiah 44:6). All those things totter and fall. Founded on nothing their end is the end of a tale that is told. Even at the golden height of most honored consistency they were founded on a wrong idea. There is a doctrine building out of a rock not seen by the eyes that have any power to see evil. It is binding all who accept it into one common knowledge, viz., the knowledge of good only.

There is a Science hewing out of the heart of Love, not studied by any mind believing in two substances. It is proclaiming Spirit unto Spirit that all do now know good and good only. The knowledge of Spirit is the only knowledge.

There is a government being wrought out of Omnipotent tenderness. Its proclamations cannot be heard by any who believe in the inferiority or superiority of one under or over another. Its pulsing strokes fall softly on the hills of anguish and in the valleys of despair: "There is no government but self-government; which is the knowledge that God is the Omnipotence within and around every creature." Whoever believes that he has a right to govern or be governed by his neighbor, cannot hear the strokes of the hammer of the Almighty. Daniel and John saw our age in symbols. We feel it in the crashings of old dynasties, or the consciousness of a triumphant doctrine which defends and provides and holds us fast, fearless at peace on its bosom — which?

June 5, 1892

LESSON XI

DWELLING IN PERFECT LIFE

Daniel 3:13-25

Napoleon said that when the reign of conscience should begin his reign would end.

So he never let even a little glint of conscience get into his mental kingdom till one day he felt a trifle sorry for his dealings with Josephine. This admission of the hint of a possibility that he could do anything that he could be sorry for opened a spot on the externals of his career where that quicksand rivulet of an idea for which he was famous could break out.

The rivulet was underground, like all the beginnings of quicksand streams. But, like all quicksand streams, it broke out on the surface. Conscience made the basin.

The quicksand stream always running within his mind was the idea what he should do in case of defeat. It broke loose instantly when he made a soft spot by being sorry for one thing he had done.

It is not always a regret for what you have done that causes the quicksand idea in your mind to break out in failure or affliction. These lessons are adapted to every kind of mind and have purposed to show you that if you have a sneaking little notion that you are not quite master of your business or of your art some unguarded word or action will give that little notion mastery over your affairs.

Even children should not get the idea that they are not yet perfect in their studies or in the art they have chosen. For, in Truth, their soul is the origin of the arts and sciences. *"Their angels do always behold the face of their Father"* (Matthew 18:10). Their inmost thoughts dwell in illuminated wisdom. To tell them this, is truer than to tell them they do not know. If you tell them that in Truth they are wise they will find some way to express outwardly what they know at the soul.

If you were nagged with the idea that you did not know and must work to know, very likely you do not think very much of what intelligence you have. This poor idea of your intelligence or of your "learning" will break out on some great day in a failure of some kind which other people will say was owing to your foolish disregard of their opinions.

No such thing. It is the time for your own opinion of yourself to break out. There is no knowing what new idea opened up the chance for the old self-depreciation to show out. Maybe it was the idea that you never would have committed that secret sin the other day or a year ago if you had not been tempted more than you could resist.

In this lesson about the fiery furnace we see how surely every mind will have victory over disaster if it has had a habit of thinking that God will bring it out right.

These three men had so ardently believed in God with them that when their belief in angry kings and their opposition to their religion broke out, their belief in God with them lifted them out alive and unhurt.

In the histories of martyrs we often read of the flames and racks not hurting them at all. Some said that fair and wondrous beings came and stood by them, touching their wounds with fingers of ecstasy.

Napoleon thought it was a supreme necessity in battle to have heavy artillery. He was mistaken. The supreme necessity is a right idea of God. These three men did not think they needed any arm to save them except their idea of God. They proved the righteousness of their idea by coming out of a very hot fire without even the smell of it on their garments.

They had for many years a sneaking little thought running under their general manner of thinking. That sneaking thought was that there was a great opposition to the true God in other people's minds. They should have faced that quicksand stream straight up just as soon as it came into their mind. For indeed there is no opposition to the true God in anyone's mind. They would never have been thrown into the furnace if they had met their early error with its noble truth.

By this lesson we see that it is a greater demonstration of godliness never to get into afflictions of any kind than to get out of great afflictions bravely. For we make our own afflictions without doubt.

Now you are thinking that the baby does not make its own afflictions, and therefore this idea is a fallacy.

In Truth the baby does not suffer at all. You imagine that it suffers. Honestly take your thought that the baby is suffering off from it and you will see it smile at once. The baby expresses one of your young thoughts that you have not been thinking very long. People who have great mental suffering by reason of thinking much that there is terrible opposition to their idea of good, see a great deal of suffering wherever they go, and they do not more than get in your house till the baby has pains and accidents to express their idea. They unite their strong belief in opposition to the good with your indifferent idea on that subject, and together you fix up the baby to scream and cry all night.

Let you both drop the idea and the baby will sleep just as its soul is resting. It will express its soul estate — the real of itself. God is Rest. It will rest. Night is the signal that we should all express the Rest of God. God is as much Rest as He is Strength.

People who have to work nights are expressing their notion of much opposition to their idea of good. If they should once see the idea that God is Rest they would be taken up as by a strong hand and put down into some resting place.

If they should go right back to their idea of there being opposition to the good and say, "There is no opposition anywhere, in all the universe, to my idea of good," they would never have any hard places to rest from. It is a high statement of Spiritual Science which Jesus Christ made, *"My yoke is easy"* (Matthew 11:30), *"Ye shall find rest"* (Jeremiah 6:16). You have been praising the martyrs, have you not? See to it that you praise their idea of the power of God to save. Do not get to thinking with them that suffering is a necessity to bring out the virtues of men. Do not get to thinking with them that the time of suffering is the time of manifestation of God's power.

Praise their idea that God will save, till by praising it you see clearly that there was nothing to be saved from except their notion that suffering is an ordinance of God. Then you will suddenly see how inspired Jeremiah was when he said that *"a man's word is His only burden"* (Jeremiah 23:36).

This third chapter of Daniel shows that there is nothing to be saved from except our own ideas. It shows that one true idea held firmly will be a golden thread of light to bring us into the realm of all Truth. One true idea in your mind will take you through into all Truth, if you will look hard at it and never mind whether you know much or little, or whether your lot is hard or easy.

For instance one of these men, who came out of a hot furnace by holding an ecstatic state of mind, was named Azariah. This name signifies that he believed strongly in God as his defense in the day of affliction. It was a truth as far as it went and out of his hot affliction he came safely.

Another of those men was entranced by the idea that all things are the free gift of God. It was the idea that:

"When earthly helpers fail,
And comforts flee.
God of the helpless,
He remembers me."

This idea was just as capable of giving him the free gift of cool breaths in names as Azariah's idea of defense. The other one was named Mishael. That name shows that he believed that his substance, the very substance of his body, was God. No one believes that fire can burn God. So whoever believes that the substance of his body is God will certainly never have any thing hurt him.

The golden text of this lesson tells us that if we will hold any one of these ideas held by these three men we will come off victorious over every trial. *"When thou walkest through the fire thou shall not be burned"* (Isaiah 43:2). Some things make up the fires through which one walks, and other things make up the fires through which others walk.

A true idea coming into mind will lift you out of your fire safely. A true idea in my mind will lift me out safely. Will lift anyone out who thinks it. One woman had a cancer on her nose which was her fire of affliction. Someone sent her a true idea of God, and it rushed through her mind like a white stream of glory and washed that cancer out in one night. Another woman had a tumor which was her hot furnace of trial. A true idea was printed in a little blue magazine in Chicago (printed by Emma Curtis Hopkins Seminary), and when she read it that idea rushed the tumor out of her body in less than twelve hours.

A man had a film on his eye, and it slipped off at the reading of an idea of God which a friend wrote him in a letter.

To these three men recorded by Daniel the idea appeared as a man. To the great King Nebuchadnezzar it looked like the "Son of God." Our ideas often stand out as beings who do not appear mortal and natural, like those we deal with in business.

This lesson suggests that we love the practice of the Presence of God. We love the marvelous. It tells us to go back to the first principle established in Universal Mind. That first principle is that, *"There is good for me."* Everything says this unconsciously. When it says it consciously the good begins to come towards it. When the mind says boldly of this good that it ought to have it, that Good hurries to meet its owner.

The word good is a little waxy subject in the mind. We can "bring forth" out of it, or "make" out of this word whatever good thing we name as what we ought to have. Watch the word good for awhile as you name it as what you ought to have. All things are made out of the word "And the Word was God." And God is Good.

There is a cord connecting your good with you. If you are anxious your anxiety is a corrosive sublimate to eat off that cord. So you must not let anxiety rest in your mind. Jesus Christ said: *"Take no thought"* (Matthew 6:25), *"Be not afraid"* (Matthew 14:27). We can stop being anxious, and stop being anxious, and stop being anxious, till everything we think we ought to have comes running swiftly to greet us.

"It shall come to pass that while they are yet speaking I will answer them" (Isaiah 65:24). The idea of opposition to our ideas of good which makes all the human hardships brought about by spreading this idea abroad, is called a "wilderness" by Ezekiel; "Lion's den" and "Fiery furnace" by Daniel. When Ezekiel was speaking of human experiences as a wilderness he said it was the

highest law to refuse the teachings of our fathers and mothers, our ministers and our school teachers. (Look into the deep meaning of Ezekiel, Twentieth chapter and eighteenth verse.) They all represent some ideas we have given great authority and prominence in our mind. Every one of them had so much trouble that they represented to us more the idea of opposition to good than power of good. Whoever believes much in opposition to his idea of good will get very blue and despondent. If he had an idea that it is his duty to work with all his might — "to widen the skins of light and make the struggle with darkness narrower," he will be a philanthropist or reformer. Then we shall praise him. But his overpowering sorrow at the sufferings of this planet makes him a very lugubrious (mournful) mentality to have around.

All the good the reformer does is by his idea that suffering can be ameliorated by his efforts, seconded by his God. That idea is very, very slim and tender by the side of his mournful idea of the power of the opposition to his God, however, and so he really fans the furnace of pain for those he would save. This lesson compels the conclusion — Nebuchadnezzar hoping — that God will save, and not the true thinker ignoring the flames. Shall the reformer and philanthropist look into the dens of crime and ignore them, according to metaphysics? He shall.

He shall not respect the sight of the eyes or the hearing of the ears, when they report pain. He shall not record the doings of misery. They are only his own long-held notions spread out in his sight. As he looks at these evidences of his own quick-sands of past thoughts taught by those who believed in opposition to good, he shall say: "I do not judge after the sight of my eyes, nor after the hearing of my ears; I judge by my idea of the Omnipresence and Omnipotence of God. Let now God be manifest here."

He shall stand by that idea and that alone, till it is his vital faith. *"According to thy faith be it unto thee"* (Matthew 9:29). Shall a poor miner, a half paid printer, a feeble sewing girl, a wounded heart, ignore the difference between their lot and the lot of a Vanderbilt or a Field? They shall. They shall look straight into the airs that are full of God and say to God alone: "Thou art my noble Comrade, my rich and powerful Champion."

They shall stand by that Truth until it is their vital faith. And they shall see God manifest, first by the unsought kindness of mankind, the unmasked comradeship of good people, the unbegged gifts of the rich, and powerful, and then by the wonderful possessions of their own, whereby they are able to lift every burden off their neighbors with wisdom of action and without sorrow. It is written that David was a man after God's own heart, simply because he spoke so richly of God and ignored everything else. Every man is after God's own heart when he tells the Truth of God.

There is no opposition to God in Truth. Speak this out boldly and see it demonstrated. Tell the child God is with him as his High Counselor, and that there is no opposition to his God. Shout it to the beggars that God is their rich and powerful Champion, and nothing can withstand Him.

Tell it to the convicts that God is their noble Comrade, and nothing can oppose Him. Ezekiel saw in his fifteenth chapter that the very best old teachings would be burned up in the fires of Truth. There shall not be a pin left in the true teachings upon which to hang our miseries. This is Bible prophecy. The only pin we can tie to is the Truth concerning God, which is first thought out as a righteous principle, and then which shows as a helper out of the troubles we are now in, and then shows as the only Presence knowing nothing of trouble any more at all.

June 12, 1892

LESSON XII

WHICH STREAK SHALL RULE

Daniel 6:16-28

Every mind has a religious streak. Every mind has a business streak. Every mind has a political streak. There is a streak of every department of human endeavor in every mind. Each one of us lets one streak or the other dominate. We can choose which streak shall rule.

Some streaks have much admiration bestowed upon them when they are prominent. Some streaks receive a great deal of censure.

When Bunyan saw a drunken thief he said: "But for the grace of God, there goes John Bunyan."

Oliver Goldsmith was very stupid at school. The streak of love of letters was not uncovered in him till something happened that uncovered that streak, and we have his inimitable books.

Something happened to you once which uncovered the streak of mechanical tendency, and you became a printer, or a stenographer, or a sewing machine operator, or maybe you are an inventor.

If you admire scholasticism, why did you not uncover that learning? You have without doubt (according to metaphysics, which is mental science as taught by Jesus Christ) as much ability to become a world-famed scholar as President Eliot and President Harper

If you admire statesmanship, why did you not uncover that streak in your reservoir? You might just as well have uncovered the streak you love and admire as the line of hiring out to your neighbors at a dollar and a half or so a day, which you know very well makes you "mad" when you think of it.

When the religious streak is uncovered, it passes through three stages if we give it freedom to be natural. If we let our religious tendency come to the surface freely, and let it spring forth from our center without hindrance of prejudice or bias, we shall get into the genius of it swiftly.

But whether we nag and cuff our religious ideas or not, they run through three stages before they, as one stream from our mind, strike the sunlit heights of miracle working.

To be doubting ourselves and speaking ill of ourselves is nagging and cuffing our genius, and has the effect of prolonging our time of travel up the mount of enchantment.

The three stages up to the point of ability to turn water into wine, make bread out of nothing, coin gold out of bones, heal sickness, raise dead people into happy life, stop pain everywhere, are hope, faith, love.

Whoever fails once in his attempt to perform a cure or carry on a ministry is tarrying at the threshold of faith or hope. He has not reached love.

Was Daniel at the court of Darius the Mede in the city of faith or of love as to his own mental state? Love is understanding. It is specially written of Daniel that he had understanding. But the name Darius means restrainer, and Daniel was his prisoner. So we know by this that Daniel was at the gateway of understanding, just ready to enter in, at 80 years of age, when Darius threw him into the den of lions (This lesson is Daniel 6).

Another way we may know that Daniel had not entered into the third stage of his religious aspiration is by the fact of his being in a den of lions and having such a pack of enemies.

Whoever has enemies does not understand God; has not struck the third round of religious ascent. Whoever gets into great trials has not entered into the delectable country of love.

Whoever has hope only will get into troubles. If he has faith he will get out of them. If he has love he will have an enchanted life, free from sorrows.

This simple division will tell you how far you have given your religious streak its liberty. For the liberty of a faculty is necessary to its perfection.

The same is true of every faculty that is true of the religious one, but the Bible Lessons are intended to show that the religious streak is the one that is capable of quickening all the others if it is allowed to leap and spring like a fountain, forth from our center.

Columbus had uncovered his idea of the sphericity of the earth. Every child ever born on the planet knew it before him, but paid no attention to his knowledge. Then there came a time when Columbus had faith.

After his discovery he had hoped that the world would rejoice in the new country. But people did not want Columbus to have so much glory and treasure, so they persecuted him. He had enemies undermining his reputation and efforts in the most subtle fashions. One night he heard a voice saying out of the darkness, "Fear not, I will provide for thee." Then his faith quickened.

In every line of endeavor there is the genius of success. The instant one strikes the round of love, or understanding of his art, he is no longer hounded, but honored.

Each faculty can call on its spirit of success to hasten it on to victory. If you are in a line you have chosen, call on the god of that art to give you victory. It is sometimes quite necessary to call the god of battles to make him triumphant, instead of on God as a principle. For a close issue, a necessity for quick action demands the close, quick action of God. This might make it seem as if there were many gods, instead of one God. No, God is one, but God acts through your line for you, and through your neighbor's line for him.

There is a God of business transactions ready to lift you into prosperity the instant you specify that it is along that line you would like Him to act.

God always works for prosperity, bounty, beauty, peace. But you might put the abstract principle to working for the dematerialization of your body before you wished to disappear, if you should spend much time praying even in a scientific fashion unto God, as God in the abstract.

We are all getting this moment exactly what we have prayed for. We get into our daily lot exactly what we have described God to be. A man had a habit of going before light every morning into a mountain and praising the wisdom and knowledge of God. It was not long before he was noted for his wisdom and drew many wise people around him.

Another man praised God as the spirit of union — unity. He declared himself married to the Spirit of God. He described God as his Provider, his Merciful Protector, his High Counselor. Thus he was miraculously provided for, carefully guided away from every danger, wise in counsel.

This was the exact opposite of the Guyon and Fenelon type of union with God. They called upon the God of safe transit through suffering. Jesus Christ taught the God of safe transit over suffering.

Bravery because of hope in God, or faith that God will save, is not high religion.

Absolute safety is the only religion worth while. The teachings of men that bravery in battle, boldness in a cause, are God-like, are humbug. In high Truth there is no one to fear, for nothing has any power to hurt and no one wants to hurt.

In high Truth we dwell at the center in safety and greatness with God. Why not tell the truth about this country through which we are walking? The whole truth instead of stopping short would astonish you. The truth is there are no lions and no den. The truth is that God is the God of Heaven, the God of safety, the God of prosperity. Try telling this story to yourself for awhile. Daniel was well enough as far as he went, but lion's dens have no charm for you. You love the stories of the mansions of goodness with harmony around you better. So does everyone.

According to the uncovered spring of the fountain of God leaping toward the sunlit heights of the companionship of Jesus, I rejoice that my High Counselor, Truth, has told me that it is a low kind of religion which teaches that God afflicts or permits afflictions and then takes us out of them that we may be thankful enough to satisfy His greed for praise.

"As I live, saith my God, I know the thoughts that I think towards you — thoughts of peace and not evil, to bring you an expected end" (Jeremiah 29:11).

See that? The expected end is always triumphant prosperity.

Knowing this awakens love. Knowing this takes away all fear. Keeping on in this knowledge is mastery over every circumstance, not by desperate struggling either as man with man to see who will beat or with God to see if we cannot win Him over, but by easy praise.

The love of God in the heart through knowing His character causes us to praise all things. They will do exactly as we want them to if we praise them with the wisdom that our high religion teaches. See how the earth pours forth grains and fruits, foliage and vegetables because the ministers in their pulpits praise the goodness of God in her.

Then see how the Russians lie down and starve, while the millions of beggars put up their wan faces in all countries, just because the ministers have taught that God is better pleased with sackcloth and ashes, hard bread and fasting, than with beautiful clothing and plenty to eat.

They have seen now the fruits of their words in full measure.

Of course scientifically, they were in the stage of hope, where the mind tries every expedient to see which will demonstrate redemption from evil. They have felt afar off that there was something wrong about our clothing and food. This was the hint of the spirit that clothing should not be made with material hands, of material substance: nor food produced by such processes. According to the high truth all clothing should fall upon us from the Beauty of Holiness, and all food should come to us from the word of God.

But neither by splendor of silks, nor by squalor of sackcloth, is the road to the raiment and food which is ours by divine right. Only by the pathway of Truth are provision and defense.

Daniel was enough inside the gateway of love so that his mind praised the lions for their obedience to him. The least little shining of love will make even the chairs in the house move around at your bidding. The mountains would move into the salt sea of the west, and lift up their rocks of protection at the command of the least little glint of the love which tips the heights of religion.

This love manifests itself in praise. You would be found praising even your debts for their goodness and tenderness and loving kindness to you. Debts are heavy burdens in the mind that has not entered the portal of love, where you can praise them till they walk away to spots where God has laid by your treasures. They really are your safe guides into prosperity.

Did you ever try praising your affairs? No? Then try telling them how you love them for their goodness. Praise them that they hold for you the secret of good. You have been hating your lot, have you not? Your lot is your lion's den. Now that you have got into it, praise the lions. Poor dumb affairs. They are not to blame. Lovingly speak to them. No matter how dry the den is, how frightened and trembling you feel. Do not play the Darius, hoping something will turn up. Be Daniel. You need not try to be brave. Just practice the words of loving kindness. Talk to your affairs as you would to a frightened child.

The cross mother frightens the child still more. The loving mother quiets it and sets it to play or to work again. A timid little woman always most afraid of dogs or anything, was always beset by dogs. (Of course she was. Whatever you fear most, will come sailing up to you by and by.) She learned this law of praise, and when once a savage dog broke his chain and sprang toward her, she touched the gateway of love just a bit and spoke to him as a masterful lover of dogs would speak, and he shrunk away to his kennel.

Daniel struck the gatepost of heaven when the lions faced him, and looked upon them in love. *"God is love"* John 4:8). *"My God hath sent His angel and hath shut up the lion's mouth"* (Daniel 6:22).

The angel that God sent to Daniel was the one that the same God has sent to you to read this lesson. That angel is named Praise. Praise your hardships. Speak tenderly to them. Take them close. The lions were friendly to Daniel. Your hardships are friendly to you.

Daniel believed in his God. "God is love." Love sends an angel to every trial. Always the angel is Praise. Not praise of a Great Being sitting on a throne, but praise of the trial. Such a friendly lion as that one is that faces you up, little mother. Tell it you do not hate it. Such a friendly lion as comes looking into your eyes, brave, hard-working father. Tell it you understand it. Such a great dumb friend is that lion, whose eyes look into yours, lonely, unprotected heart. Look him straight in the eyes. Tell him God's angel of praise walks beside you.

In Spiritual Science we do not think it a sign of much knowledge of God to have troubles come upon us, but we know there is always a sure and swift and merciful way out, if we have got into them.

Here you perceive living troubles are called lions. Last Sunday, diseases and sicknesses were meant by fires. You have heard many a woman and man say that living troubles are the worst of all troubles, have you not? Well, that is where some living people have got you in their power in some (seemingly; remember, there is no reality in trouble, though while it seems real it is just as hard to bear). People have you in their power if they have any power to hurt you, if they have any hold on your lot to wound you by what they do.

This lesson is for such conditions. It teaches that you face the condition square-up — the debt itself, not the one you owe — the grief itself, not the one who grieves you — the shame itself, not the one who shames you. Those who do you wrong are Darius. The feeling that faces you, or the thing they do, is the lion. What you say to the situation will fix the situation. Then, when the situation yields, "They have no power to hold you or hurt you forevermore."

"The love of God constraineth me" (2 Cor. 5:14). "How can I keep from singing about the angel abiding with me, closing all the lions' mouths, into whose den I have been so foolish as to fall?" This is the way you feel long before your friends who have yielded to the temptation to hurt you, feel sorry like Darius, that they failed you just when you needed them most.

We are not called to martyrdom of any kind, but being in it let us take the Daniel way out.

We must take a good stand regarding our religious streak. It seems that Jesus Christ was positive that we get all the graces, if that streak dominates. Daniel was sure of it. Moses was sure of it. Moses and Daniel could not help getting into trouble. Jesus said He took our troubles voluntarily to show the highest way out of every sort and kind thereof.

By His methods He tacitly praised both Daniel and Moses, but by His tears at the grave of Lazarus He showed that Martha and Mary and Lazarus would have given higher evidence of understanding Him if they had kept alive and well instead of getting sick and dying.

To let the scholastic streak loose in us is to become pedantic, lean, dry as dust, and rheumaticky. The highest honors of men will be awarded us. But what are they worth?

To let the philosophic and speculative streak loose is to become cold and critical, intellectual and unmerciful. We shall get the praises of our own generation and the reverence of posterity. But what are those worth?

To let the management of finances loose is to have thousands of men and women and children by the throats, and to be cowered before by our neighbors, whose labor we are buying. We shall find mayhap, some great institution which believes in the absence of God, and a great monument may crumble in some noble city to mark our resting place. But what is that worth?

Jesus Christ said, *"The fashion of this world passeth away"*

(Corinthians 7:31), *"My words are Life..."* (John 6:63), *"I am the Truth"* (John 14:6).

Come back here to the foundation whence the living waters flow. It is not too late to begin all over again, uncovering the living stream of the religious faculty which wells in every mind.

And then, if we but let the stream flow freely, untravelled by the ideas of even the martyrs, hope will quickly clasp hands with faith, and love will chant victory over sin, death, and the grave.

On the white wings of Truth fly, 'soul of man'.
June 19, 1892

LESSON XIII

SEE THINGS AS THEY ARE

Review of 12 Lessons

Astronomers tell us that we see points of light in the skies which we name stars, that are the lights of globes long vanished from the heavens. It takes light so long to travel that we have only just received the radiance they sent forth ages ago.

Metaphysicians tell us that we are just now seeing people in the light or shade of ways we used to think. We may have ceased to believe the imaginations of our youth, but the beliefs of that time often proceed forth from us and cover some person or circumstance with our imagination of them, which they ought not to be judged by.

It is the province of the knowledge of Absolute Truth to cause us to see things as they are; not through our predilections. It may happen to one who has carried a heavy grief for twenty years that some idea enters the mind which takes out the core of the grief, and yet the mind will sometimes feel mournful on the shades of the memory of how the heart used to grieve. One often loves or fears on the shadow of what he used to feel positively.

Religionists tell us that the world lay in the night of deep darkness till Jesus, the Sun of Righteousness, arose and broke the night with the glory of His life. And now all the ignorance and misfortune we experience are but the broken memories of a night long since erased.

Material things and human experiences are all the symbols of thoughts. The thought that there is a mixture of goodness and evil in the universe may have been reasoned out of our mind, and yet what we used to think about good and evil being sadly mixed may now cover the ways of our neighbors or the state of the world with what seems to us to be a very bad state of affairs. If so we must get rid of the "shades of the departed." In Truth there is a way to be rid of them.

All belief in astrals is the remnant of darkness of mind. All coverings of people with our past ideas are astrals. Let us be rid of astrals. Let us look back upon Alpha and forward to Omega. God, the Lover and Friend; God, the Keeper and Protector; God, the Provider and Inspiration; is behind us and before us. This is Truth.

There are some ideas that come into the mind and stay there as embedded as slivers in the flesh or bullets shot into undeliverable places. An instance of how stories will penetrate and shed abroad their effects is here in point.

A young lady was reading in a Spiritual Science lesson of a man who had kept saying "The Lord is your keeper," till the words had saved a child from the hurt of an accident. The accident took place minus its hurt. The beautiful text, "The Lord is your keeper," found a lodgment in her mind. There it lay ready to spring forth when an opening should be made for it. The opening came when the train on which she was riding ran off an embankment. Suddenly like a living creature the text sprang from her mind and caught the baggage car in such a position that the coaches were saved. No one was hurt.

"Thy words are Life to them that find them" (Proverbs 4:22). *"Truth is a shield and buckler"* (Psalm 91:4). *"The Truth shall make you free"* (John 8:32).

It was mentioned in a recent magazine that for the last fifteen years drunkenness and crime had been terribly on the increase. The whole plan was then made plain whereby the innocent holders of horrible stories are the shedders abroad of temptation.

For just about fifteen years the eloquent crusaders against vice have transfixed impressionable audiences with stories of wickedness, which they have unconsciously projected, as the beautiful words, "The Lord is your keeper," flew on its mission.

What kind of stories do you fix into the minds of the people you meet? Ideas are living things. They are caged lions of prowess. They are projectiles from small bore rifles or heavy caliber guns.

The Bible Lessons for the last quarter have been loaded with ideas whose purpose and sure results are to cause those who have read them under the light of Truth to be workers for the redemption of mankind from its imaginations of evil. You who have carried one single idea around with you, whose reasonableness and grandeur have captured, have stopped some lie on someone's lips before it was uttered; have caused some hand about to strike to fall down; have taken the sting out of some cup; have withdrawn the drowsiness from some brain.

Which of them has appealed to you most out of the last quarter's mine of golden texts? This being a review, let us name them. They are the radiance of stars in the firmament of Jehovah, and of their glory there is no end. The stars of the night may fall from their bright places, and the suns of the invisible heights may be darkened ere their first beams strike our planet; but the words of Eternal Truth shall go on and the hearts that love them shall rise on their wings of light out of the reach of sin, death and pain.

The first one was April the third (this quarter). Its point was, that you attract people who represent your thoughts; as Socrates said that grief would attract sickness, waste of property and death.

A young metaphysician suddenly discovered that being with one who was a reliable healer of sickness, he caught a state of Mind quite different from what he had been holding, and it was efficient to cure without his making any effort. He said he just left his mind free to take on the strong lights and shades of other people's minds, and knowing just how to drop their errors he could keep their virtues. He noticed that being prosperous is entirely a state of mind. He is now practicing being near prosperous people so that he may minister the quality of mentality that draws prosperity when he walks among the wretched. He means to get so strong in the idea of the providing bounty of the Almighty that stones of poverty cannot stick in his mind, no matter how real they may seem to others nor even if some great preacher describes them.

While training to be strong on the side of power, health, loving kindness, do not tell anyone your experiences. Self-feed and self-increase with Truth. Truth told before you are positive as the archangel may be so argued down that you feel as weak in spirit as a rag of nothingness. Jesus Christ said: *"See thou tell no man"* (Matthew 8:4).

Remember that methods count for nothing. If you are in the proper state of mind you might as well sell warming pans in the Torrid Zone, like

Lord Timothy Dexter, as to sell lace at $100 per yard, like Steward or Fields (stores in Chicago).

You certainly must have noticed how some people are lucky, anyhow. That is because they have a mind that attracts luck. This Science teaches one how to attract good into his life. It is a good doctrine to preach to the disconsolate. God is the feeder and healer and companion, according to this doctrine, and nothing is too small a situation or state of affairs for His goodness to pay close attention to. If you stop to think of it, no one is so prosperous and wise as Jehovah. That is why we are advised to talk with Him much. Misfortune and ignorance cannot stay in His presence. Stop often and commune with the Owner of Worlds.

The next was that all kinds of divorce came from the dark belief once started that God is without, and not within. It dropped its shades down over men till they thought other people could get the advantage over them, so they fell to fighting them. This was warfare on the battlefield and in the home. Did you ever think that many a martial hero got his prowess from the brave fight his mother made with that fate which she believed had given her husband the advantage against her?

Why did she not rise and proclaim that God is both within and without, since God is everywhere? The Jehovah within the feeblest little woman is the Jehovah without in the husband she fears or the legislation against her. Who shall prevail against the Omnipotent God?

Now, the idea that God is within us, not without us, is just as divorcing as the other that He is without, not within, for it gets us to feeling able to get ourselves healthy, but gets us into tangles with the outside world. It withdraws us from our fellow men and makes hermits of us. We get to thinking that people do not understand us. We get a multitude of feelings which separate us from people.

The third lesson was the injunction not to feel responsible for anything; to let God take the responsibility. *"At destruction and famine thou shalt laugh"* (Job 5:22). They tell you that the cars have run off the track and killed a hundred. According to God it is no such thing. The whole thing is the shadow of an idea which never was true. So laugh in your soul and silently tell your High Counselor you do not believe He ever let such an event happen in His beautiful kingdom. Then you will do and say to the messenger the right thing. Many will be suddenly helped into healing and life. Turn to your Comrade, Jehovah, when they report evil concerning your home, your prospects, your friends. Tell Him, "I know Thy goodness towards me. How Thou dost glorify me continually."

The fourth tells us to practice every night and very early in the morning, telling the Spirit of God that we never made any mistakes, because God being our mind and our life, mistakes in that mind and life are impossible. Then through the day act from the standpoint of having done very wisely always. Take it for granted that methods do not count. Nothing counts except our relation with God. If one has *"wasted his substance in riotous living"* (Luke 15:13), and feels downhearted, he is to tell the Spirit that there cannot be any waste in Truth, because all comes from God and goes to God.

"Omnipresence none can flee,
Flight from God to God must be."

One who had formerly been too economical for any use got up from the table and burned a plate of doughnuts, saying, "I praise you for your increasing Substance, food from the table of God. Wherever the airs blow this smoke there someone will kindly feed a neighbor."

To her hearers it sounded like superstition. They thought she had gone daft. No, she was spreading the healing word. Her stinginess was broken down. She had to do something exactly opposite to her stinginess. *"My ways are not your ways, saith the Lord"* (Isaiah 55:8).

The fifth tells us that we must learn to get our living in some other way than earning it by the sweat of our brow by hiring out to our neighbors.

The result of that idea that got embedded into mind ages ago that man must labor in a material fashion is that now it is almost impossible for the laboring classes to rest a moment without suffering for it. The average wages for an adult are $1.02 per day. He pays rent at the rate of four or five times what the same home would have been a few years ago, and the poor man's taxes are out of all proportion to the capitalist's taxes.

It is the result of the curse or lie concerning labor. Jesus said, *"Labor not for the meat that perisheth"* (John 6:27). He advised looking to God for clothing and food. All the shiftlessness of mankind, all the weariness of them, all the discouragement, are from ceasing to expect the Almighty to provide. Therefore this lesson advised all the world to put up its hands and receive from the invisible Hand of our everlasting Parent all its provisions.

Every single morning at some particular hour, tell the Spirit that you do not look to any enterprise or to any human being for your provisions, but to the Spirit only. Then go on as usual about your daily tasks, till the Hand of Love stretches down and changes your lot. There is a change of affairs belonging to every child on this planet.

"Let's take by faith while living,
Our freehold by thanksgiving."

The only labor enjoined according to Jesus Christ is thanksgiving to the Omnipotent God, *"My yoke is easy"* (Matthew 11:30), He said. Here we find that it will soon be made utterly impossible for one to get more goods than his neighbor. The truth concerning our God as our Provider will equalize all things. Caste will be abolished; not by anarchy, but by prayer. Labor and capital will soon be erased; not by fighting, but by thanksgiving to God. The morning that dawned on Galilee's waters is just falling on my lot and on your lot. God is here.

The sixth tells about Satan. It shows that all the satan there is or ever was is our subconscious thought that after all, maybe God intends for us to be afflicted somehow. While the preacher is praising up his God for being so good to him, he is secretly thinking how often God has seen fit to afflict him or his family "in His inscrutable Providence." All subconscious or secret thoughts come to the surface in home, business, friendships, positions among mankind. Many a poor minister or half mankind. Many a poor minister or half-starved pietist may lay his decrepitude and misery to his own reserved opinion concerning God. Each one must face up this satan of thinking, "What if evil should be my portion whether I call upon God or not?" Meet Satan promptly. Jesus Christ is the antidote to Satan. Look your vague terror in the face with the name, Jesus Christ. That Name means the visibility of God.

The seventh shows that if you know what is true according to the Life of the Spirit, your knowing is like a river set flowing. One does not have to strive to carry out his Truth by stopping his factory when he hears that all clothing should be made out of the Word of Truth. He does not have to close up the schoolhouse when he learns that all schools are founded on the lie concerning the absence of intelligence. No, he sees that his

***knowledge is all the power he needs to exercise. He need not stop eating to show how long his God will keep him alive without food. His knowledge will regulate his actions. No man should give up anything by force of human will. All should be accomplished by the irresistible action of the Principle. The action of Spirit is as positive with us when we hear it as it was when it struck Saul to the earth.

The Supreme Truth that is now being believed by so many people is flowing through the bodies and homes and affairs of men like a river. Away over the horizons, into the abysses of a forgotten dream, are all the former ways being washed.

"And the former heaven and the former earth shall be forgotten; neither shall they come into mind anymore" (Revelations 21:4).

The eighth shows that the science of mathematics, of stars, of stones, of chemistry, is as helpless to provide against earthquakes, tidal waves, lightnings, plagues, cyclones, as the simple Indian's sure prognostications that these things are coming. Only the Science of Spirit annuls calamity. This lesson shows that our boasted civilization is the mixed iron and clay age spoken of by Daniel. We have had our golden height of sincerity that man is ruled over by his brother man by right of inheritance from God. This has descended into the scramble for power on every hand. We have had the golden head of conviction that some men are given more judgment from

Jehovah than others. This has descended into the systems of cramming with masses of teachings that are foolishness with God.

We have had our golden height of sincere believing that the church was instituted for the salvation of souls, which has now descended into the flinching and cringing of the preachers in the face of death and disease, as powerless to hush as the schools. The scramble of the religious for salaries and honors in common with the believers in material methods is the mixture of clay and iron. And all the time the hammers of the true kingdom are sounding on the ears of those who know that the Spirit of God is in every man equally as in his neighbor, so that there is no need of any government save the knowledge of Spirit. This age closes the reign of intellect and matter. The sciences of the schools shall not count us in hand for this kingdom only so far as they wear down the intellect to acknowledging that the most it knows is that it knows nothing. To study the sciences of the schools chafes the brain into inflammation and softness. The study of the Science of Spirit quickens the intelligence to know what was and is and shall be. The ears can hear the sound of the voices of the workmen hewing out the mansions for those who do not mix their knowledge that there is no soul to save, for God is the only Soul, with the former idea of salvation.

The ninth and tenth show that we never need to face up people who have done us injuries, but we are to look the injuries straight in the face and get right with them, after which it will be easy enough to get on with our fellow men and women. Paul and Peter and James saw this, but not so plainly as these lessons bring out.

Tell those troublesome affairs that they are your kind and loving friends with ability to go right to the treasure house where your rightful inheritance is, and bring you your rights at once. Love them and praise them. The other side of them is delight. They will fly to the places whence your help can come easily. The first thing you do after praising them is right. You were not intended to be burdened, or sick, or ignorant, or unfortunate, or abused. These states of situations need praising, and loving and directing, not hating, and repelling and striking. They are angels of goodness in disguise. Talk to them wisely. Never mind people. Keep your world under your feet, not on your back, nor in your arms.

The last is all about keeping your own counsel. If the Spirit tells you to go and heal a dying case, do not tell of it. Go and do as you are bidden and come again bringing your triumphs. If the Spirit bids you rest, obey and ask no odds of any man. If you are given to spreading your spoken words concerning your secret with God you will be saved so as by fire. That which is true of the world at large, preach boldly. What the Spirit gives you alone keep as the secret of the Lord. The Spirit intends for you to cure everyone and raise everyone to Life when it whispers to you. It does not come to take you by the hand through tribulations, but out of the reach of them.

There is a particular way for you to get out of that difficulty you are now in. Keep counsel with no one save the powerful Champion, the Lord God of Sabaoth (hosts, armies). Thou shalt hear a voice behind thee saying: *"This is the way; walk ye in it"*(Isaiah 30:21).

June 26, 1892.

Notes

Other Books by Emma Curtis Hopkins

- *Class Lessons of 1888 (WiseWoman Press)*
- *Bible Interpretations (WiseWoman Press)*
- *Esoteric Philosophy in Spiritual Science (WiseWoman Press)*
- *Genesis Series*
- *High Mysticism (WiseWoman Press)*
- *Self Treatments with Radiant I Am (WiseWoman Press)*
- *Gospel Series (WiseWoman Press)*
- *Judgment Series in Spiritual Science (WiseWoman Press)*
- *Drops of Gold (WiseWoman Press)*
- *Resume (WiseWoman Press)*
- *Scientific Christian Mental Practice (DeVorss)*

Books about Emma Curtis Hopkins and her teachings

- *Emma Curtis Hopkins, Forgotten Founder of New Thought* – Gail Harley
- *Unveiling Your Hidden Power: Emma Curtis Hopkins' Metaphysics for the 21st Century (also as a Workbook and as A Guide for Teachers)* – Ruth L. Miller
- *Power to Heal: Easy reading biography for all ages* –Ruth Miller

To find more of Emma's work, including some previously unpublished material, log on to:

www.emmacurtishopkins.com

WiseWoman Press

1521 NE Jantzen Ave #143
Portland, Oregon 97217
800.603.3005
www.wisewomanpress.com

Books Published by WiseWoman Press

By Emma Curtis Hopkins

- *Resume*
- *Gospel Series*
- *Class Lessons of 1888*
- *Self Treatments including Radiant I Am*
- *High Mysticism*
- *Esoteric Philosophy in Spiritual Science*
- *Drops of Gold Journal*
- *Judgment Series*
- *Bible Interpretations: Series I, II, III, IV, V, and VI*

By Ruth L. Miller

- *Unveiling Your Hidden Power: Emma Curtis Hopkins' Metaphysics for the 21st Century*
- *Coming into Freedom: Emily Cady's Lessons in Truth for the 21st Century*
- *150 Years of Healing: The Founders and Science of New Thought*
- *Power Beyond Magic: Ernest Holmes Biography*
- *Power to Heal: Emma Curtis Hopkins Biography*
- *The Power of Unity: Charles Fillmore Biography*
- *Uncommon Prayer*
- *Spiritual Success*
- *Finding the Path*

Watch our website for release dates and order information! - www.wisewomanpress.com

List of Bible Interpretation Series

with date from 1st to 14th Series.

This list is complete through the fourteenth Series. Emma produced at least thirty Series of Bible Interpretations.

She followed the Bible Passages provided by the International Committee of Clerics who produced the Bible Quotations for each year's use in churches all over the world.

Emma used these for her column of Bible Interpretations in both the Christian Science Magazine, at her Seminary and in the Chicago Inter Ocean Newspaper.

First Series

July 5 - September 27, 1891

Lesson 1	The Word Made Flesh	July 5th
	John 1:1-18	
Lesson 2	Christ's First Disciples	July 12th
	John 1:29-42	
Lesson 3	All Is Divine Order	July 19th
	*John 2:1-1*1 (Christ's first Miracle)	
Lesson 4	Jesus Christ and Nicodemus	July 26th
	John 3:1-17	
Lesson 5	Christ at Samaria	August 2nd
	John 4:5-26 (Christ at Jacob's Well)	
Lesson 6	Self-condemnation	August 9th
	John 5:17-30 (Christ's Authority)	
Lesson 7	Feeding the Starving	August 16th
	John 6:1-14 (The Five Thousand Fed)	
Lesson 8	The Bread of Life	August 23rd
	John 6:26-40 (Christ the Bread of Life)	
Lesson 9	The Chief Thought	August 30th
	John 7:31-34 (Christ at the Feast)	
Lesson 10	Continue the Work	September 6th
	John 8:31-47	
Lesson 11	Inheritance of Sin	September 13th
	John 9:1-11, 35-38 (Christ and the Blind Man)	
Lesson 12	The Real Kingdom	September 20th
	John 10:1-16 (Christ the Good Shepherd)	
Lesson 13	In Retrospection	September 27th
		Review

Second Series

October 4 - December 27, 1891

Lesson 1	Mary and Martha *John 11:21-44*	October 4th
Lesson 2	Glory of Christ *John 12:20-36*	October 11th
Lesson 3	Good in Sacrifice *John 13:1-17*	October 18th
Lesson 4	Power of the Mind *John 14:13; 15-27*	October 25th
Lesson 5	Vines and Branches *John 15:1-16*	November 1st
Lesson 6	Your Idea of God *John 16:1-15*	November 8th
Lesson 7	Magic of His Name *John 17:1-19*	November 15th
Lesson 8	Jesus and Judas *John 18:1-13*	November 22nd
Lesson 9	Scourge of Tongues *John 19:1-16*	November 29th
Lesson 10	Simplicity of Faith *John 19:17-30*	December 6th
Lesson 11	Christ is All in All *John 20: 1-18*	December 13th
Lesson 12	Risen With Christ *John 21:1-14*	December 20th
Lesson 13	The Spirit is Able Review of Year	December 27th

Third Series

January 3 - March 27, 1892

Lesson 1	A Golden Promise *Isaiah 11:1-10*	January 3rd
Lesson 2	The Twelve Gates *Isaiah 26:1-10*	January 10th
Lesson 3	Who Are Drunkards *Isaiah 28:1-13*	January 17th
Lesson 4	Awake Thou That Sleepest *Isaiah 37:1-21*	January 24th
Lesson 5	The Healing Light *Isaiah 53:1-21*	January 31st
Lesson 6	True Ideal of God *Isaiah 55:1-13*	February 7th
Lesson 7	Heaven Around Us *Jeremiah 31 14-37*	February 14th
Lesson 8	But One Substance *Jeremiah 36:19-31*	February 21st
Lesson 9	Justice of Jehovah *Jeremiah 37:11-21*	February 28th
Lesson 10	God and Man Are One *Jeremiah 39:1-10*	March 6th
Lesson 11	Spiritual Ideas *Ezekiel 4:9, 36:25-38*	March 13th
Lesson 12	All Flesh is Grass *Isaiah 40:1-10*	March 20th
Lesson 13	The Old and New Contrasted Review	March 27th

Fourth Series

April 3 - June 26, 1892

Lesson 1	Realm of Thought *Psalm 1:1-6*	April 3rd
Lesson 2	The Power of Faith *Psalm 2:1-12*	April 10th
Lesson 3	Let the Spirit Work *Psalm 19:1-14*	April 17th
Lesson 4	Christ is Dominion *Psalm 23:1-6*	April 24th
Lesson 5	External or Mystic *Psalm 51:1-13*	May 1st
Lesson 6	Value of Early Beliefs *Psalm 72: 1-9*	May 8th
Lesson 7	Truth Makes Free *Psalm 84:1-12*	May 15th
Lesson 8	False Ideas of God *Psalm 103:1-22*	May 22nd
Lesson 9	But Men Must Work *Daniel 1:8-21*	May 29th
Lesson 10	Artificial Helps *Daniel 2:36-49*	June 5th
Lesson 11	Dwelling in Perfect Life *Daniel 3:13-25*	June 12th
Lesson 12	Which Streak Shall Rule *Daniel 6:16-28*	June 19th
Lesson 13	See Things as They Are Review of 12 Lessons	June 26th

Fifth Series

July 3 - September 18, 1892

Lesson 1	The Measure of a Master *Acts 1:1-12*	July 3rd
Lesson 2	Chief Ideas Rule People *Acts 2:1-12*	July 10th
Lesson 3	New Ideas About Healing *Acts 2:37-47*	July 17th
Lesson 4	Heaven a State of Mind *Acts 3:1-16*	July 24th
Lesson 5	About Mesmeric Powers *Acts 4:1-18*	July 31st
Lesson 6	Points in the Mosaic Law *Acts 4:19-31*	August 7th
Lesson 7	Napoleon's Ambition *Acts 5:1-11*	August 14th
Lesson 8	A River Within the Heart *Acts 5:25-41*	August 21st
Lesson 9	The Answering of Prayer Acts 7: 54-60 - Acts 8: 1-4	August 28th
Lesson 10	Words Spoken by the Mind *Acts 8:5-35*	September 4th
Lesson 11	Just What It Teaches Us *Acts 8:26-40*	September 11th
Lesson 12	The Healing Principle Review	September 18th

Sixth Series

September 25 - December 18, 1892

Lesson 1	The Science of Christ *1 Corinthians 11:23-34*	September 25th
Lesson 2	On the Healing of Saul *Acts 9:1-31*	October 2nd
Lesson 3	The Power of the Mind Explained *Acts 9:32-43*	October 9th
Lesson 4	Faith in Good to Come *Acts 10:1-20*	October 16th
Lesson 5	Emerson's Great Task *Acts 10:30-48*	October 23rd
Lesson 6	The Teaching of Freedom *Acts 11:19-30*	October 30th
Lesson 7	Seek and Ye Shall Find *Acts 12:1-17*	November 6th
Lesson 8	The Ministry of the Holy Mother *Acts 13:1-13*	November 13th
Lesson 9	The Power of Lofty Ideas *Acts 13:26-43*	November 20th
Lesson 10	Sure Recipe for Old Age *Acts 13:44-52, 14:1-7*	November 27th
Lesson 11	The Healing Principle *Acts 14:8-22*	December 4th
Lesson 12	Washington's Vision *Acts 15:12-29*	December 11th
Lesson 13	Review of the Quarter	December 18th
Partial Lesson	Shepherds and the Star	December 25th

Seventh Series

January 1 - March 31, 1893

Lesson 1	All is as Allah Wills	January 1st
	Ezra 1	
	Khaled Knew that he was of The Genii	
	The Coming of Jesus	
Lesson 2	Zerubbabel's High Ideal	January 8th
	Ezra 2:8-13	
	Fulfillments of Prophecies	
	Followers of the Light	
	Doctrine of Spinoza	
Lesson 3	Divine Rays Of Power	January 15th
	Ezra 4	
	The Twelve Lessons of Science	
Lesson 4	Visions Of Zechariah	January 22nd
	Zechariah 3	
	Subconscious Belief in Evil	
	Jewish Ideas of Deity	
	Fruits of Mistakes	
Lesson 5	Aristotle's Metaphysician	January 27th
	Missing (See Review for summary)	
Lesson 6	The Building of the Temple	February 3rd
	Missing (See Review for summary)	
Lesson 7	Pericles and his Work in building the Temple	
	Nehemiah 13	February 12th
	Supreme Goodness	
	On and Upward	
Lesson 8	Ancient Religions	February 19th
	Nehemiah 1	
	The Chinese	
	The Holy Spirit	
Lesson 9	Understanding is Strength Part 1	February 26th
	Nehemiah 13	
Lesson 10	Understanding is Strength Part 2	March 3rd
	Nehemiah 13	
Lesson 11	Way of the Spirit	March 10th
	Esther	
Lesson 12	Speaking of Right Things	March 17th
		Proverbs 23:15-23
Lesson 13	Review	March 24th

Eighth Series

April 2 - June 25, 1893

Lesson 1	The Resurrection	April 2nd
	Matthew 28:1-10	
	One Indestructible	
	Life In Eternal Abundance	
	The Resurrection	
	Shakes Nature Herself	
	Gospel to the Poor	
Lesson 2	Universal Energy	April 9th
	Book of Job, Part 1	
Lesson 3	Strength From Confidence	April 16th
	Book of Job, Part II	
Lesson 4	The New Doctrine Brought Out	April 23rd
	Book of Job, Part III	
Lesson 5	The Golden Text	April 30th
	Proverbs 1:20-23	
	Personification Of Wisdom	
	Wisdom Never Hurts	
	The "Two" Theory	
	All is Spirit	
Lesson 6	The Law of Understanding	May 7th
	Proverbs 3	
	Shadows of Ideas	
	The Sixth Proposition	
	What Wisdom Promises	
	Clutch On Material Things	
	The Tree of Life	
	Prolonging Illuminated Moments	
Lesson 7	Self-Esteem	May 14th
	Proverbs 12:1-15	
	Solomon on Self-Esteem	
	The Magnetism of Passing Events	
	Nothing Established by Wickedness	
	Strength of a Vitalized Mind	
	Concerning the "Perverse Heart"	

Lesson 8	Physical vs. Spiritual Power	May 21st
	Proverbs 23:29-35	
	Law of Life to Elevate the Good and Banish the Bad	
	Lesson Against Intemperance	
	Good Must Increase	
	To Know Goodness Is Life	
	The Angel of God's Presence	
Lesson 9	Lesson missing	May 28th
	(See Review for concept)	
Lesson 10	Recognizing Our Spiritual Nature	June 4th
	Proverbs 31:10-31	
	Was Called Emanuel	
	The covenant of Peace	
	The Ways of the Divine	
	Union With the Divine	
	Miracles Will Be Wrought	
Lesson 11	Intuition	June 11th
	Ezekiel 8:2-3	
	Ezekiel 9:3-6, 11	
	Interpretation of the Prophet	
	Ezekiel's Vision	
	Dreams and Their Cause	
	Israel and Judah	
	Intuition the Head	
	Our Limited Perspective	
Lesson 12	The Book of Malachi	June 18th
	Malachi	
	The Power of Faith	
	The Exercise of thankfulness	
	Her Faith Self-Sufficient	
	Burned with the Fires of Truth	
	What is Reality	
	One Open Road	
Lesson 13	Review of the Quarter	June 25th
	Proverbs 31:10-31	

Ninth Series

July 2 - September 27, 1893

Lesson 1	Secret of all Power	July 2nd
Acts 16: 6-15	The Ancient Chinese Doctrine of Taoism	
	Manifesting of God Powers	
	Paul, Timothy, and Silas	
	Is Fulfilling as Prophecy	
	The Inner Prompting.	
	Good Taoist Never Depressed	
Lesson 2	The Flame of Spiritual Verity	July 9th
Acts 16:18	Cause of Contention	
	Delusive Doctrines	
	Paul's History	
	Keynotes	
	Doctrine Not New	
Lesson 3	Healing Energy Gifts	July 16th
Acts 18:19-21	How Paul Healed	
	To Work Miracles	
	Paul Worked in Fear	
	Shakespeare's Idea of Loss	
	Endurance the Sign of Power	
Lesson 4	Be Still My Soul	July 23rd
Acts 17:16-24	Seeing Is Believing	
	Paul Stood Alone	
	Lessons for the Athenians	
	All Under His Power	
	Freedom of Spirit	
Lesson 5	(Missing) Acts 18:1-11	July 30th
Lesson 6	Missing No Lesson *	August 6th
Lesson 7	The Comforter is the Holy Ghost	August 13th
Acts 20	Requisite for an Orator	
	What is a Myth	
	Two Important Points	
	Truth of the Gospel	
	Kingdom of the Spirit	
	Do Not Believe in Weakness	

Lesson 8	Conscious of a Lofty Purpose	August 20th
Acts 21	As a Son of God	
	Wherein Paul failed	
	Must Give Up the Idea	
	Associated with Publicans	
	Rights of the Spirit	
Lesson 9	Measure of Understanding	August 27th
Acts 24:19-32	Lesser of Two Evils	
	A Conciliating Spirit	
	A Dream of Uplifting	
	The Highest Endeavor	
	Paul at Caesarea	
	Preparatory Symbols	
	Evidence of Christianity	
Lesson 10	The Angels of Paul	September 3rd
Acts 23:25-26	Paul's Source of Inspiration	
	Should Not Be Miserable	
	Better to Prevent than Cure	
	Mysteries of Providence	
Lesson 11	The Hope of Israel	September 10th
Acts 28:20-31	Immunity for Disciples	
	Hiding Inferiorities	
	Pure Principle	
Lesson 12	Joy in the Holy Ghost	September 17th
Romans 14	Temperance	
	The Ideal Doctrine	
	Tells a Different Story	
	Hospitals as Evidence	
	Should Trust in the Saviour	
Lesson 13	Review	September 24th
Acts 26-19-32	The Leveling Doctrine	
	Boldness of Command	
	Secret of Inheritance	
	Power in a Name	

Tenth Series

October 1 – December 24, 1893

Lesson 1	*Romans 1:1-19*	October 1st
	When the Truth is Known	
	Faith in God	
	The Faithful Man is Strong	
	Glory of the Pure Motive	
Lesson 2	*Romans 3:19-26*	October 8th
	Free Grace.	
	On the Gloomy Side	
	Daniel and Elisha	
	Power from Obedience	
	Fidelity to His Name	
	He Is God	
Lesson 3	*Romans 5*	October 15th
	The Healing Principle	
	Knows No Defeat.	
	In Glorified Realms	
	He Will Come	
Lesson 4	*Romans 12:1*	October 22nd
	Would Become Free	
	Man's Co-operation	
	Be Not Overcome	
	Sacrifice No Burden	
	Knows the Future	
Lesson 5	*I Corinthians 8:1-13*	October 29th
	The Estate of Man	
	Nothing In Self	
	What Paul Believed	
	Doctrine of Kurozumi	
Lesson 6	*I Corinthians 12:1-26*	November 5th
	Science of The Christ Principle	
	Dead from the Beginning	
	St. Paul's Great Mission	
	What The Spark Becomes	
	Chris, All There Is of Man	
	Divinity Manifest in Man	
	Christ Principle Omnipotent	

Lesson 7	*II Corinthians 8:1-12*	November 12th
	Which Shall It Be?	
	The Spirit is Sufficient	
	Working of the Holy Ghost	
Lesson 8	*Ephesians 4:20-32*	November 19th
	A Source of Comfort	
	What Causes Difference of Vision	
	Nothing But Free Will	
Lesson 9	*Colossians 3:12-25*	November 26th
	Divine in the Beginning	
	Blessings of Contentment	
	Free and Untrammeled Energy	
Lesson 10	*James 1*	December 3rd
	The Highest Doctrine	
	A Mantle of Darkness	
	The Counsel of God	
	Blessed Beyond Speaking	
Lesson 11	*I Peter 1*	December 10th
	Message to the Elect	
	Not of the World's Good	
Lesson 12	*Revelation 1:9*	December 17th
	Self-Glorification	
	The All-Powerful Name	
	Message to the Seven Churches	
	The Voice of the Spirit	
Lesson 13	Golden Text	December 24th
	Responding Principle Lives	
	Principle Not Hidebound	
	They Were Not Free Minded	
Lesson 14	Review	December 31st
	It is Never Too Late	
	The Just Live by Faith	
	An Eternal Offer	
	Freedom of Christian Science	

Eleventh Series

January 1 – March 25, 1894

Lesson 1	*Genesis 1:26-31 & 2:1-3*	January 7th
	The First Adam	
	Man: The Image of Language Paul and Elymas	
Lesson 2	*Genesis 3:1-15*	January 14th
	Adam's Sin and God's Grace	
	The Fable of the Garden	
	Looked-for Sympathy	
	The True Doctrine	
Lesson 3	*Genesis 4:3-13*	January 21st
	Types of the Race	
	God in the Murderer	
	God Nature Unalterable	
Lesson 4	*Genesis 9:8-17*	January 28th
	God's Covenant With Noah	
	Value of Instantaneous Action	
	The Lesson of the Rainbow	
Lesson 5	I Corinthians 8:1-13	February 4th
	Genesis 12:1-9	
	Beginning of the Hebrew Nation	
	No Use For Other Themes	
	Influence of Noble Themes	
	Danger In Looking Back	
Lesson 6	*Genesis 17:1-9*	February 11th
	God's Covenant With Abram	
	As Little Children	
	God and Mammon	
	Being Honest With Self	
Lesson 7	*Genesis 18:22-23*	February 18th
	God's Judgment of Sodom	
	No Right Nor Wrong In Truth	
	Misery Shall Cease	
Lesson 8	*Genesis 22:1-13*	February 25th
	Trial of Abraham's Faith	
	Light Comes With Preaching	
	You Can Be Happy NOW	

Lesson 9	*Genesis 25:27-34*	March 4th
	Selling the Birthright	
	"Ye shall be Filled"	
	The Delusion Destroyed	
Lesson 10	*Genesis 28:10-22*	March 11th
	Jacob at Bethel	
	Many Who Act Like Jacob	
	How to Seek Inspiration	
	Christ, the True Pulpit Orator	
	The Priceless Knowledge of God	
Lesson 11	*Proverbs 20:1-7*	March 18th
	Temperance	
	Only One Lord	
	What King Alcohol Does	
	Stupefying Ideas	
Lesson 12	*Mark 16:1-8*	March 25th
	Review and Easter	
	Words of Spirit and Life	
	Facing the Supreme	
	Erasure of the Law	
	Need No Other Friend	

Twelfth Series

April 1 – June 24, 1894

Lesson 1	*Genesis 24:30, 32:09-12*	April 8th
	Jacob's Prevailing Prayer	
	God Transcends Idea	
	All To Become Spiritual	
	Ideas Opposed to Each Other	April 1st
Lesson 2	*Genesis 37:1-11*	
	Discord in Jacob's Family	
	Setting Aside Limitations	
	On the Side of Truth	
Lesson 3	*Genesis 37:23-36*	April 15th
	Joseph Sold into Egypt	
	Influence on the Mind	
	Of Spiritual Origin	
Lesson 4	*Genesis 41:38-48*	April 22nd
	Object Lesson Presented in	
	the Book of Genesis	
Lesson 5	*Genesis 45:1-15*	April 29th
	"With Thee is Fullness of Joy"	
	India Favors Philosophic Thought	
	What These Figures Impart	
	The Errors of Governments	
Lesson 6	*Genesis 50:14-26*	May 6th
	Changes of Heart	
	The Number Fourteen	
	Divine Magicians	
Lesson 7	*Exodus 1:1-14*	May 13th
	Principle of Opposites	
	Power of Sentiment	
	Opposition Must Enlarge	
Lesson 8	*Exodus 2:1-10*	May 20th
	How New Fires Are Enkindled	
	Truth Is Restless	
	Man Started from God	
Lesson 9	*Exodus 3:10-20*	May 27th
	What Science Proves	
	What Today's Lesson Teaches	
	The Safety of Moses	

Lesson 10	*Exodus 12:1-14*	June 3rd
	The Exodus a Valuable Force	
	What the Unblemished Lamp Typifies	
	Sacrifice Always Costly	
Lesson 11	*Exodus 14:19-29*	June 10th
	Aristides and Luther Contrasted	
	The Error of the Egyptians	
	The Christian Life not Easy	
	The True Light Explained	
Lesson 12	*Proverbs 23:29-35*	June 17th
	Heaven and Christ will Help	
	The Woes of the Drunkard	
	The Fight Still Continues	
	The Society of Friends	
Lesson 13	*Proverbs 23:29-35*	June 24th
	Review	
	Where is Man's Dominion	
	Wrestling of Jacob	
	When the Man is Seen	

Thirteenth Series

July 1 – September 30, 1894

Lesson 1	The Birth of Jesus	July 1st
	Luke 2:1-16	
	No Room for Jesus	
	Man's Mystic Center	
	They glorify their Performances	
Lesson 2	Presentation in the Temple	July 8th
	Luke 2:25-38	
	A Light for Every Man	
	All Things Are Revealed	
	The Coming Power	
	Like the Noonday Sun	
Lesson 3	Visit of the Wise Men	July 15th
	Matthew 1:2-12	
	The Law Our Teacher	
	Take neither Scrip nor Purse	
	The Star in the East	
	The Influence of Truth	
Lesson 4	Flight Into Egypt	July 22nd
	Mathew 2:13-23	
	The Magic Word of Wage Earning	
	How Knowledge Affect the Times	
	The Awakening of the Common People	
Lesson 5	The Youth of Jesus	July 29th
	Luke2:40-52	
	Your Righteousness is as filthy Rags	
	Whatsoever Ye Search, that will Ye Find	
	The starting Point of All Men	
	Equal Division, the Lesson Taught by Jesus	
	The True Heart Never Falters	
Lesson 6	The "All is God" Doctrine	August 5th
	Luke 2:40-52	
	Three Designated Stages of Spiritual Science	
	Christ Alone Gives Freedom	
	The Great Leaders of Strikes	
Lesson 7	Missing	August 12th
Lesson 8	First Disciples of Jesus	August 19th
	John 1:36-49	
	The Meaning of Repentance	

	Erase the Instructed Mind	
	The Necessity of Rest	
	The Self-Center No Haltered Joseph	
Lesson 9	The First Miracle of Jesus	August 26th
	John 2:1-11	
	"I Myself am Heaven or Hell"	
	The Satan Jesus Recognized	
	The Rest of the People of God	
	John the Beholder of Jesus	
	The Wind of the Spirit	
Lesson 10	Jesus Cleansing the Temple	September 2nd
	John 2:13-25	
	The Secret of Fearlessness	
	Jerusalem the Symbol of Indestructible Principle	
	What is Required of the Teacher	
	The Whip of Soft Cords	
Lesson 11	Jesus and Nicodemus	September 9th
	John 3:1-16	
	Metaphysical Teaching of Jesus	
	Birth-Given Right of Equality	
	Work of the Heavenly Teacher	
Lesson 12	Jesus at Jacob's Well	September 16th
	John 4:9-26	
	The Question of the Ages	
	The Great Teacher and Healer	
	"Because I Live, Ye shall Live Also."	
	The Faith That is Needful	
Lesson 13	Daniel's Abstinence	September 23rd
	Daniel 1:8-20	
	Knowledge is Not All	
	Between the Oriental and Occidental Minds	
	The Four Servants of God	
	The Saving Power of Good	
	The Meeting-Ground of Spirit and Truth	
Lesson 14	Take With You Words	September 30th
	John 2:13-25	
Review	Healing Comes from Within	
	The Marthas and Marys of Christianity	
	The Summing up of The Golden Texts	

Fourteenth Series

October 7 – December 30, 1894

Lesson 1	Jesus At Nazareth	October 7th
Luke 4:16-30	Jesus Teaches Uprightness	
	The Pompous Claim of a Teacher	
	The Supreme One No Respecter of Persons	
	The Great Awakening	
	The Glory of God Will Come Back	
Lesson 2	The Draught of Fishes	October 14th
Luke 5:1-11	The Protestant Within Every Man	
	The Cry of Those Who Suffer	
	Where the Living Christ is Found	
Lesson 3	The Sabbath in Capernaum	October 21st
Mark 1:21-34	Why Martyrdom Has Been a Possibility	
	The Truth Inculcated in Today's Lesson	
	The Injustice of Vicarious Suffering	
	The Promise of Good Held in the Future	
Lesson 4	The Paralytic Healed	October 28th
Mark 2:1-12	System Of Religions and Philosophy	
	The Principle Of Equalization	
	The Little Rift In School Methods	
	What Self-Knowledge Will Bring	
	The Meaning Of The Story of Capernaum	
Lesson 5	Reading of Sacred Books	November 4th
Mark 2:23-38	The Interior Qualities	
Mark 2:1-4	The Indwelling God	
	Weakness Of The Flesh	
	The Unfound Spring	
Lesson 6	Spiritual Executiveness	November 11th
Mark 3:6-19	The Teaching Of The Soul	
	The Executive Powers Of The Mind	
	Vanity Of Discrimination	
	Truth Cannot Be Bought Off	
	And Christ Was Still	
	The Same Effects For Right And Wrong	
	The Unrecognized Splendor Of The Soul	

Lesson 7	Twelve Powers Of The Soul	November 18th
Luke 6:20-31	The Divine Ego in Every One	
	Spiritual Better than Material Wealth	
	The Fallacy Of Rebuke	
	Andrew, The Unchanging One	
Lesson 8	Things Not Understood Attributed to Satan	
Mark 3:22-35	True Meaning Of Hatha Yoga	November 25th
	The Superhuman Power Within Man	
	The Problem of Living and Prospering	
	Suffering Not Ordained for Good	
	The Lamb in the Midst shall Lead	
Lesson 9	Independence of Mind	December 2nd
Luke 7:24-35	He that Knoweth Himself Is Enlightened	
	The Universal Passion for Saving Souls	
	Strength From knowledge of Self	
	Effect Of Mentally Directed Blows	
Lesson 10	The Gift of Untaught wisdom	December 9th
Luke 8:4-15	The Secret Of Good Comradeship	
	The Knower That Stands in Everyone	
	Laying Down the Symbols	
	Intellect The Devil Which Misleads	
	Interpretation Of The Day's Lesson	
Lesson 11	The Divine Eye Within	December 16th
Matthew 5:5-16	Knowledge Which Prevails Over Civilization	
	The Message Heard By Matthew	
	The Note Which shatters Walls Of Flesh	
Lesson 12	Unto Us a Child I s Born	December 23rd
Luke 7:24-35	The Light That is Within	
	Significance Of The Vision of Isaiah	
	Signs of the Times	
	The New Born Story Of God	
	Immaculate Vision Impossible To None	
Lesson 13	Review	December 30th
Isaiah 9:2-7	That Which Will Be Found In The Kingdom	
	Situation Of Time And Religion Reviewed	
	Plea That Judgment May Be Righteous	
	The Souls Of All One And Changeless	

Made in the USA
Charleston, SC
25 May 2011